Securing the Salvation of Your Children

Mark Van Bever

DEDICATION

This book is lovingly dedicated to the millions of children who need to know Jesus and to their parents who have the responsibility to be part of the process to pass the baton of faith to those children.

It is especially dedicated to my wife Margy, who helped me to lay a foundation for our son Stephen's salvation and to Stephen and his wife, Kristin, who are laying a foundation for their children's salvation.

TABLE OF CONTENTS

INTRODUCTION

There is a tendency in America today for Christian parents to turn over many of the responsibilities concerning their children to other adults. Day care workers serve as stand in parents who have had much of the rearing process passed on to them. In doing so, the shaping of our children's morals and social skills is largely out of our control.

This passing of responsibilities is not limited to moral and social training only. We have handed down our children's spiritual training in the same manner. Our church teachers have become our children's primary source of information about God and Christian values. Those few minutes of training each week are not enough.

I am not saying that day care workers and church teachers are unqualified, but I do want to say that Christian parents need to take an active role in the child training process. Our precious children have been entrusted to us for a short while, and we will be accountable to God for our efforts in training them to be Christ-like.

"Train up a child in the way he should go, even when he is old he will not depart from it." (Proverbs 22:6)

It is your responsibility to do the training. It is your responsibility to teach your children to be Christ-like. It is your responsibility to commit to be an active part of "SECURING THE SALVATION OF YOUR CHILDREN."

PRECONCEPTION ACTIVITIES (BEFORE CONCEPTION)

The process of securing your child's salvation begins with you. Absolutely, God must draw your child to Him before your child can be saved, but you should lay a foundation for God's drawing.

The parent, who is responsible for training his child, must already be trained. I would not think of teaching someone to play the piano because I have never learned. If I offered piano lessons, the students would leave the class and still be untrained.

A child is a student who needs to be trained in the things of God, and the parent is the teacher. Before your child is conceived, be prepared to teach him about Jesus and lead him to salvation. It is important to be prepared because you are accountable to God concerning how well you teach your child.

It is one thing for me to try to teach piano and have the students leave the class untrained, but it is far more serious for you to try to teach your child about salvation and have him leave childhood untrained. Train yourself to be a capable teacher. Your child's eternal destiny may depend on you.

The ideal time for a pastor to learn to deliver a sermon is before it is time to preach, and the ideal time for a school teacher to learn to instruct students is before class begins. Similarly, the ideal time to know how to lead a child to salvation is before he is on board and ready to be led. I suggest that the ideal time is before he is ever conceived.

Just as it takes years of study and practice to be a school teacher or a pastor, it takes years of training to become skilled at leading children to Christ. The process is more than the thirty minutes required to share the gospel with a child and pray with him to receive Jesus as Lord.

You will have to "show" him the Christian life for five to twelve years before it is time for those precious thirty minutes. This book will discuss those thirty minutes, but the main objective is to cover the years of preparation crucial to arriving at sharing the *"...light of the gospel of the glory of Christ..." (2 Corinthians 4:4)*

If the process of securing your child's salvation begins with you, and the ideal starting point is preconception, what can you do before conception to prepare yourself?

1. Experience Salvation Yourself

Your child will need to know that salvation makes him feel sure that heaven awaits him. He will need to hear how God's love can be his comfort when he hurts. He should be told about the joys of Christian friendship.

To share these benefits of salvation genuinely and adequately, you must have experienced salvation yourself. Almost everyone who reads this book will be a Christian who is eager to lead her or his child into a personal relationship with Jesus, but if you are not a Christian, I urge you to study Romans 10:9-10 and seek counseling from a Christian pastor.

Salvation results from believing and confessing that Jesus died to take the penalty of your sins, and He was raised from the dead in victory over those sins. It is essential for you to experience salvation for yourself, if you are going to train your child to desire salvation for himself.

There was a water park a couple of hours from my home, which my wife and I enjoyed very much. It had a pool, slides of all kinds, a wave making machine, rapids, and a sunning area. I have experienced that park and can, therefore, tell of its delights. When my son was old enough, I passed on to him my experiences and persuaded him to come to the park, also.

Experience the joy of discovering eternal life. Encounter a God Who is strength in time of weakness and help in time of need. Receive the encouragement that God causes to leap out of the Bible. Experience salvation yourself so you can tell of its delights and pass it on to your child, persuading him to come to God, also.

2. Put Your Spiritual Life in Order

People are three-part beings. We have a spirit, we possess a soul (mind, will, emotions), and we live in a body. Each part is important and must be cared for.

We spend a lot of time caring for our bodies. The body is cleaned, fed, and exercised. It is primped and pampered to look its best. We are very body conscious.

The mind is cared for well, also. Education is valued highly, and a keen mind is a decided advantage in our society. We want to have will power and well-controlled emotions. We are soul conscious.

While the body and mind are paid much attention, the spirit is often neglected. We forget that our essence is a spirit in the image of God. Our body and soul may get tired and stop, but our spirit lives on eternally in heaven or hell. "... *Though our outer*

man is decaying, yet our inner man is being renewed day by day."
(2 Corinthians 4:16)

The spirit is the part of us that fellowships with God. *"God is spirit; and those who worship Him must worship in spirit and truth." (John 4:24)* Our spirit can be developed to better fellowship with God.

Spend time in prayer, training yourself to communicate with God. There will be many times you will want to talk to God about your child. You will want to talk about his health, friends, school work, and emotional development. Train yourself to talk to God before those times arrive.

Develop the habit of daily Bible study. Just as the body needs food to be active and strong, the spirit needs nourishment if it is to be strong. The food of the spirit is God's word. *"Man does not live on bread alone, but on every word that proceeds out of the mouth of God." (Matthew 4:4)* Feast your spirit on God's Word.

In addition to personal prayer and Bible study, you should develop your spirit by establishing a family devotion time. Pick a time that suits your schedule and refine a format that you will follow.

With toddlers, I have experienced success by inventing a devotion from a favorite story book. When Jack falls down and breaks his crown, point out that God can make him better, and then pray for Jack. Children's books have a lot of nature pictures. Present a devotion that teaches your child that God made the bunnies, trees, and flowers that are in his books.

For children attending school, I suggest the format begin by reading from a good children's daily devotion book. This should be followed by a time encouraging discussion of the devotional reading. Finally, close the session with prayer centered around the content of the reading. A good format length is fifteen minutes or less depending on the child's age. This is long enough to make a point without over stressing the attention span.

Prayer, Bible study, and family devotions will accomplish two purposes. They will develop your spirit and put order into your spiritual life. A strong spirit puts you in position to direct your child toward Jesus.

The process of putting your spiritual life in order also involves your other two parts, the body and mind. Your entire being needs to be submitted and committed to God if you are going to reach your potential in being able to secure the salvation of your children.

Romans 12:1-2 says, "I urge you therefore, brethren, by the mercies of God, to present your bodies a living and holy sacrifice, acceptable to God, which is your spiritual service of worship. And do not be conformed to this world, but be transformed by the renewing of your mind, that you may prove what the will of God is, that which is good and acceptable and perfect."

The body is addressed first. You are to present your body a living and holy sacrifice. A sacrificial animal was brought to the altar and left there for God to use in any way He desired. The owner of the animal gave up all rights to the sacrifice.

You are urged to give your body to God to be used in any way He desires. As you present your body to Him, you give up all rights to use it selfishly for your desires. In these ways, you are like the animal sacrifice, but there is an important difference.

The animal sacrifice could only be offered once, because death was involved. You are to be a living sacrifice, which can be offered over and over to God for His service. One of those services is to secure your child's salvation. Become proficient at presenting your body to God so that you are ready to be used in the service of saving your child.

Your spirit is put in order through prayer and Scripture study, and your body is put in order through presenting it to God as a living sacrifice. The third part of you, your soul (mind, will, emotions) must be put in order, too.

Romans 12:2 tells us that a part of the soul, the mind, is transformed through a renewal process. Your mind must be renewed to think in line with God's Word. Renewal of the mind takes place through conscientious Scripture intake. Notice the importance of Scripture in putting your spiritual life in order. Purposeful time in God's Word orders both the spirit and the soul.

The soul has been trained to think like the world. The soul has been taught to fear, worry, and doubt. It puts trust in man's ability and not God's ability. A retraining or renewal process is necessary so that the soul begins to think like God.

The soul that is not renewed thinks contrary to God's Word. When it is 10:00 p.m. and your spouse is not home from church, you may imagine an auto accident instead of believing that God is in control and using your spouse to help someone.

When you fail at something, you may perceive yourself as no good instead of relying on God to help you succeed the next time. When you have the sniffles, you may see yourself as sick tomorrow instead of completely well tomorrow. Our thinking process needs to be renewed.

James 1:21 says *"... in humility receive the Word implanted, which is able to save your souls."* James is writing to fellow Christians explaining how their minds can be saved from worldly training. When he uses the word "soul", he is not talking about accepting Jesus as Lord and being saved because he uses the Greek word that means mind, psyche. Psyche is the root of our word psychology, the study of the mind. James is addressing the renewal of the minds of those who are already Christians.

It is true that the Word will lead a person to a rebirth of his or her spirit, but here James is talking about the mind. Receiving the Word implanted can renew your mind. By studying God's word, your mind will be retrained to think in a God-like manner. This will be a vital step if you are to successfully show your child what the Christian life is like.

Your mind must be renewed to accept responsibility for leading your child to salvation. That renewal is accomplished by thinking in line with God's Word. Proverbs 22:6 tells you to train your child. The mind, once renewed to accept the God ordained responsibility of training your children, is ready to be taught to handle the responsibility successfully.

Renewal of the mind does not happen overnight. It is often a lengthy and strenuous process requiring much discipline and perseverance. Be patient with yourself and persevere. When the going gets tough, ask yourself, "Is my child's eternal salvation worth the effort?" Answer back, "Of course it is."

Put all parts of your spiritual life in order. Develop your spirit through prayer and Scripture study. Submit your body by presenting it repeatedly as a living sacrifice. Renew your mind to think in line with God's Word. Accomplish these things even before conception, and then continually improve the order of your spiritual life. Put your spiritual life in order, so you will know how to help your child order his.

3.Build Your Faith on God's Word

Romans 10:17 says, *"So faith comes by hearing and hearing by the Word of Christ."* This verse tells you how faith is built. It comes from hearing or reading God's Word from the Bible, a sermon, a teaching, a conversation, a recording, the radio, or the television.

Faith is built insufficiently through attention to God's Word on Sunday only. Notice that Romans 10:17 says we build faith from "hearing and hearing." It takes repetitive hearing or reading to build faith. The word hearing is in the continuous sense, and the verse could accurately be translated, faith is built from being continually in God's Word.

For Olympic long-distance runners to be victorious, they must continually practice. They must run when they do not want to run and put forth effort when they would rather rest. For Christians to be victorious, they must continually be in God's Word. They must put forth effort when they would rather rest.

Read the Bible story of Noah being delivered because of his obedience to build the ark. Consider Daniel, who God protected from the lions because Daniel was faithful. Look at the blessing of wisdom given to Solomon. Remember Abraham and Sarah having a son because God said they would, even though it was physically impossible. Read about the woman who was sick eighteen years, and Jesus told her, *"...Daughter, your faith has made you well; go in peace and be healed of your affliction."*

The Bible is full of accounts that will build your faith. Let them convince you that God takes care of His children. He protects them and gives them wisdom. He makes the impossible happen for His children, and He provides health. Spend time with God's Word because faith comes from hearing and reading it.

It will take effort for you to spend time in God's Word. It will take discipline to turn off the television to work at building your faith, but that is the life to which Christians are called.

Faith is a necessity for two reasons. First, "...All things are possible to him who believes." (Mark 9:23) Nothing is impossible where faith is present. Secondly, "... without faith it is impossible to please Him (God)." (Hebrews 11:6)

If you want God's realm of possibilities opened to you and you want to please Him, you must have faith. God has made His Word available to you, and now it is up to you to make *"faith come by hearing and hearing."*

Sometimes, raising your children will seem like an impossibility, but, *"All things are possible to him who"* has faith. You may feel inadequate in transferring your values to your children, but *"All things are possible to him who"* has faith. You may feel unable to be God's instrument in securing your child's salvation, but, *"All things are possible to him who"* has faith.

Build your faith even before conception, by being continually in God's Word. Strong faith will be invaluable in securing your child's salvation. That faith will also help you and your spouse through the pregnancy, the delivery, and the adjustment to having a new family addition.

Operating in faith makes securing your child's salvation a possibility. Faith also causes your efforts to be successful and pleasing to God. Build your faith on God's Word.

4. Pray for Wisdom

James 1:5 says, "But if any of you lacks wisdom, let him ask of God, who gives to all men generously and without reproach, and it will be given to him." God is faithful, and we can count on Him to give us the wisdom we ask of Him.

Much wisdom is required to properly lead a child to the point of accepting Jesus as Savior. You are the one who will need that wisdom. "And that from childhood you have known the sacred writings which are able to give you the wisdom that leads to salvation through faith which is in Christ Jesus." (2 Timothy 3:15)

Your wisdom led you to salvation, and your wisdom can help lead your child to salvation. It is your task to share your wisdom with your child. Notice that the Scriptures are able to give wisdom *"from childhood"*.

There is plenty of man-made wisdom available. Some of which is in accordance with Scripture, but there is no substitute for godly wisdom. Godly wisdom comes directly from the Father and reveals a piece of His knowledge. If you need advice, there is no better source than God.

There is a big difference between man's wisdom and God's wisdom. "This wisdom (man's wisdom) is not that which comes down from above, but is earthly, natural, demonic... But the wisdom from above is first pure, then peaceable, gentle, reasonable, full of mercy and good fruits, unwavering, without hypocrisy." (James 3:15, 17)

Human wisdom is not dependable because the insight of God is not behind it. *"There is a way which seems right to a man, but its end is the way of death." (Proverbs 16:25)* If you trust solely in your own wisdom in raising your children, the end is the way of failure, but if you rely on God's wisdom the result is abundant fruit.

Look at the fruits of God's wisdom in James 3:17. Its first effect on your mind is to make it pure. The result is to make you upright, sincere, and unstained by the world's impure thoughts. God's wisdom enables you to lead your children toward holiness.

Secondly, God's wisdom is *"then peaceable"*. It will reveal to you how to establish a peaceful environment in your home, in which your children will learn tranquil relationships. It will shelter your children from the adverse effects of turmoil on young minds.

A peaceful environment also promotes the idea of a quiet time with God.

Thirdly, God's wisdom causes a home environment to be gentle and reasonable. It is one thing to have a peaceful home because of the iron hand of a dictator, but a wonderful thing to have peace because everyone is treated gently and reasonably. Fair treatment of your children will breed trust in you that can lead them to place trust in your God.

Next, wisdom from above causes you to be merciful. It shows you how to respond to your children with love, understanding, and forgiveness; the same way God responded in mercy to His children by sending Jesus. Your mercy will cause your children to understand God's mercy when they are older.

Finally, when God imparts wisdom, the path of action becomes clear. You can guide your children without wavering. Because the path is clear, you can avoid hypocrisy by living what you are saying.

There will be many circumstances you will face with your child where God's advice will be useful, if not essential. The way you handle those circumstances will become part of the bridge between your child and God, by showing him the way God helps you with decisions. It is critically important to get ready to build the bridge before your child is born.

Wisdom is as important to a strong family as the concrete foundation is to a strong house. "By wisdom is a house built, and by understanding it is established; and by knowledge the rooms are filled with all precious and pleasant riches." (Proverbs 24:3, 4)

Develop the habit now of praying for wisdom in your daily affairs. Later, when you need guidance concerning disciplining, spiritual training, sibling rivalry, adolescence, or sex education, you will naturally go to God for wisdom. A loving and directing parent reveals the character of "the" loving and directing parent, the Father. Pray for wisdom now.

5. Learn to Hear from God

When you pray for wisdom, the answer is received by hearing from God. God may attempt to send wisdom through a book, a sermon, the words of a friend, or an inward assurance. To receive the wisdom, you must learn to hear and recognize God's attempts to speak to you.

Before conception, learn to hear from God, so that later God can drop parenting advice into your spirit. *"The spirit of man is the candle of the Lord." (Proverbs 20:27)* Physical light can be put on a subject through a candle, and spiritual light can be put on a subject through man's candle, his spirit. Man's spirit is God's channel for shedding light.

Your spirit must be unblocked by the flesh and the mind so communications can come through. At one time, our dishwasher was not draining the water when the wash cycle was complete. I discovered that the hose that transmits water to the plumbing was blocked so that the water could not get through. As soon as the hose was cleared of the things that did not belong, the transmission of water was perfect.

God is faithful to transmit, but a person dominated by fleshly desires or possessing a mind filled with worldly thoughts will block the transmission. God's voice cannot get through. As soon as fleshly desires and worldly thoughts are removed, transmission will be perfect. You must remove the things that do not belong that block transmission.

God always is transmitting, but you must have your receiver on and be tuned in, free of any interference that would block communication. It is your responsibility to remove the things in your life that cause interference.

John 10:27 says, *"My sheep hear My voice and I know them and they follow me."* A sheep hears and recognizes the voice of the shepherd if it is near the shepherd. If a sheep wanders from the shepherd, no matter how loudly the shepherd calls, the sheep does not hear.

A daily quiet time with God, the Shepherd, will put you near Him where His voice can be heard. When His voice is heard a few times, you will learn to recognize it. Then, if you are obedient to put action to the wisdom you have heard from God, you will guide your children properly.

Godly guidance will reveal the character of God to your child. He will grow up learning to desire direction. It will be a natural response for him to want to trust God for direction because of the confidence he has in you.

Remove any hindrances to communication from your life. Develop closeness to God through a quiet time. Be a listening sheep. Learn to hear from God now, so that when you need wisdom you can pray and hear.

So far, we have discussed five areas that are important in securing your child's salvation: 1. Experience salvation yourself; 2. Put your spiritual life in order; 3. Build your faith on God's Word; 4. Pray for wisdom; and 5. Learn to hear from God.

All five prepare you to minister to your child. They prepare you to raise him during the crucial first years of his life in a manner that will direct him to God. By watching you portray the character of God, he will later understand the God you introduce to him.

We have discussed these five areas in the preconception chapter because they are the foundation of securing your child's salvation. They prepare you to accomplish the responsibility. Ideally, they should be mastered before your child is conceived, but if you are past that point, start today. It is not too late.

There are at least three other areas that are ideally taken care of before conception. These areas relate to your home environment and the conception itself.

6. Be Financially Ready

Part of your responsibility as a parent will be to provide for your children financially. *"But if any one does not provide for his own, and especially those of his household, he has denied the faith, and is worse than an unbeliever." (1 Timothy 5:8)* Being ready for the additional expenses that your child will bring will prevent the stressful environment that financial problems cause.

Eighty percent of divorces are money related. Financial problems can destroy a family, causing a child to live in an environment void of the security and stability she needs. It is worth the sacrifice to clean up your money messes and be financially ready before conception.

Pay off the charge cards and get all your bills current. Talk to someone who is familiar with "new born" expenses, and put together a budget including those expenses. If possible, remove one parent's paycheck from the budget, so he or she can stay home and raise the child according to your values.

Practice living by that budget, so you develop wise spending habits. Then, when you are financially ready, be fruitful and multiply. You will offer your child an atmosphere free of the financial stresses that cause worry, arguing, and family splits.

A child is a precious gift from God. Be financially ready, and please God by providing a home suitable for caring for that gift.

7. Pray for Your Child's Physical Conception

The previous six areas of preparation concern getting you ready. Now, we will look at preparation focused on your child, specifically his conception. Christians should make it a practice to talk to God about almost everything, and your child's conception is no exception. The talking is done through prayer.

You can have confidence that God will answer when you ask in prayer. "And this is the confidence which we have before

Him, that, if we ask anything, according to His will, He hears us and if we know that He hears us in whatever we ask, we know that we have the requests which we have asked from Him." (1 John 5:14-15)

Part of your parental responsibility is to pray for your child. Start praying for him from the time you desire to conceive him, knowing that God will answer.

My wife was run over by a car when she was in college, and the doctors told her she would never have children. Four years after the accident we met, and a year later we were married. After three years of marriage, we decided to attempt to have a child, despite what the doctors said.

We prayed for God to be involved in the conception and to cause a miracle. We asked God to allow us to have a child, and six weeks later we found out that God had accomplished the impossible. Our son, Stephen, was the result. I am convinced that God wants you to pray for your child even before he is conceived. Involve God from the beginning.

When you pray, ask for more than pregnancy. Ask for conception to take place the way God designed it. Ask for a perfect beginning for your child. Ask that the mother's body will be prepared to accept the child and that the child will find security in her growing place.

God wants to be involved in the conception and subsequent growth of your child. Your responsibility is to invite Him into the process by asking in prayer. *"...You do not have because you do not ask." (James 4:2) "... ask, and you will receive, that your joy may be made full." (John 16:24)* Pray for your child's conception and God will make your joy full.

8. Pray for Your Child's Spiritual Conception

A child is a spiritual being created in the image of God. She has a mind and lives in a body, but her essence is spirit. One day the mind will stop, and the body will be shed in death, but the spirit will live on forever.

John 4:24 tells us that God is a spirit. *"God is spirit; and those who worship Him must worship in spirit and truth."* Gen.1:26 says that God decided to make man in His image, which is spirit. *"Then God said, Let Us make man in Our image, according to Our likeness..."People* are created in the likeness of God with our essence being spirit, not body.

God is vitally concerned with the spirit of people. The spirit is the part of Adam that died when he sinned. The spirit is what God redeemed through Jesus' death. The spirit of your child is what will live forever with, or apart from, God. The spirit is the real person that remains when the outer shell is gone.

Sex is so highly regulated in the Bible because it produces a spirit that never dies. Before the physical conception of your child, pray for the conception of his spirit. We focus easily on the physical part of a child, but even more attention must be given to the spirit.

Your child can fellowship with and worship God only through her spirit. *"God is spirit; and those who worship Him must worship in spirit and truth." (John 4:24)* The conception and development of her spirit is crucial to securing her salvation. It is through her spirit that she will contact and embrace Jesus as Lord.

Pray for a spirit that is sensitive to godly things and finds satisfaction in righteousness. Ask God to create a spirit that yearns for a relationship with Him. Ask God to protect your child's spirit as she grows. More and more it is accepted that a child's spirit is born at the point of conception and is shaped by experiences in the womb, so pray from the beginning.

The real birth of your child is nine months before the event we normally call birth. Pray for his essence, his spirit, to be formed properly. We will discuss the development of his spirit in the next chapter.

SUMMARY

The process of securing your child's salvation truly does begin with you and should begin even before your child is conceived. Preparing yourself to be the instrument that God will use to introduce your child to eternal life will require effort. Getting your finances in order may require sacrifice. Praying for the conception of your child's body and spirit may seem different or strange. The preconception tasks are not easy, but they lay the foundation for securing your child's salvation.

You will need discipline, determination, and perseverance. You will need a vision of what you are working toward, so that you do not quit. Visualize your child coming to Jesus through your efforts. That should be sufficient motivation for you to be prepared before conception.

PRENATAL ACTIVITIES (DURING PREGNANCY)

In the previous chapter we discussed preconception activities that lay a foundation of preparation for securing your child's salvation. We covered eight tasks to accomplish even before conception:

Preconception
1. Experience salvation yourself
2. Put your spiritual life in order
3. Build your faith on God's Word
4. Pray for wisdom
5. Learn to hear from God
6. Be financially ready
7. Pray for your child's physical conception
8. Pray for your child's spiritual conception

In this chapter, we will look at prenatal (before birth) activities, tasks to accomplish during the pregnancy period. I have listed the eight preconception tasks above because the pregnancy period is the time to finalize any that were not completed before conception.

I want to reemphasize the importance of laying a solid foundation before your child arrives. When you have dinner guests, you spend hours preparing for a meal that will last a few minutes. Everything is ready before the guests arrive, because you want the evening to be a success.

The preconception and prenatal activities are the preparation for your child's arrival. Be ready before your special guest arrives because the results of your efforts do not last just a few minutes. The results are eternal, so you must be successful.

As you proceed through the nine prenatal months, realize that your child was born at conception, and you are already a parent. You may not see your child, but he is there, and he is totally dependent on you. The time has come when your actions begin to directly affect your child's salvation.

There are many activities you can perform during the months between conception and birth that will give your child a head start toward salvation. Take them seriously because, even now, your actions have a direct impact on moving your child down the path to eternal life. Keep a vision that what you are doing is in preparation for the decision your child will make years later concerning acceptance or rejection of Jesus.

When you can't see immediate results, there is, sometimes, a tendency to be less diligent or to quit. Have faith to know that God is hearing your prayers and honoring your efforts, even though results are not visible to your sight. *"For we walk by faith, not by sight." (2 Corinthians 5:7)*

Now, let's explore some prenatal activities, keeping in mind that, even though results are not seen immediately, these activities are securing your child's salvation.

1. Lay Hands on Your Baby and Pray

Prayer is the foundation for every successful Christian endeavor. Prayer brings God on the scene before you begin, so that He is involved in the whole process. When God is part of the foundation, the results of an endeavor are solid and successful.

Securing your child's salvation is, perhaps, the most important Christian endeavor you will ever undertake. In that light, make prayer the foundation of each day, asking God to guide you into actions that will bring success in leading your child to Him. Be in prayer consistently, not just in a crisis. Pray for your child before his physical birth, not just when there is a storm later in his life.

The State of Florida is known for hurricanes during the Fall of the year. I can remember, as a boy, bolting plywood over our glass doors, getting ready before the storm. Sheets of plywood are not easily handled in 100-mile-per-hour winds and driving rain, so it was important to be prepared before the storm.

Prayer is the preparation for coming storms. God's Word asks you to *"pray without ceasing". (1 Thessalonians 5:17)* If you obey His words by establishing a foundation of prayer, then you will withstand the storms.

24 Therefore, everyone who hears these words of Mine, and acts upon them, may be compared to a wise man, who built his house on the rock.
25 And the rain descended, and the floods came, and the winds blew, and burst against that house; and yet it did not fall, for it had been founded on the rock.
26 And everyone who hears these words of Mine, and does not act upon them, will be like a foolish man, who built his house upon the sand.

27 And the rain descended, and the floods came, and the winds blew, and burst against that house; and it fell and great was its fall." (Matthew 7:24-27)

God's Word says, *"pray without ceasing"*. The meaning is to stay in an attitude of prayer. If you act on His Words and pray, your endeavors are founded on the Rock. If you do not act on His words, the fall may be great. Pray for your child during the prenatal period so that his life has a rock-solid foundation.

The point of contact between you and your child is your hands. Love, warmth, and care are transmitted through the hands. The mother, especially, has ample opportunity to contact the baby she is carrying. When you pray for your child, place your hands on him.

The laying on of hands may seem strange to you, but it is an elementary Christian doctrine to do so. "Therefore, leaving the elementary teaching about the Christ, let us press on to maturity, not laying again a foundation of repentance from dead works and of faith toward God, of instruction about washings, <u>and laying on of hands</u>, and the resurrection of the dead and eternal judgment." (Hebrews 6:1, 2)

Using the hands in prayer is not just for the mature, but a basic act for all Christians. Just as we are comfortable with teaching about Christ, repentance and eternal judgment, the laying on of hands should feel natural to us. Because the laying on of hands is foreign to many, let us explore it briefly with the goal of achieving understanding, which will allow you to be comfortable in laying hands on your child.

The practice of the laying on of hands goes back to the beginning of the Old Testament. Exodus 29:10 reads, *"Then you shall bring the bull before the tent of meeting, and Aaron and his sons shall lay their hands on the head of the bull."* Transmission took place through the hands. The sins of the men were passed to the sacrificial bull, and the perfection of the sacrifice was received, by faith, by those that laid hands on the bull. God established the laying on of hands for the benefit of people.

In the church today, the laying on of hands is used for the ordination of ministers (pastors, elders, deacons, etc.), as it was in the first century church. "And while they were ministering to the Lord and fasting, the Holy Spirit said, 'Set apart for Me Barnabas and Saul for the work to which I have called them.' Then, when they had fasted and prayed and laid their hands on them, they sent them away." (Acts 13:2,3)

The practice of laying on of hands should extend beyond the ordination ceremony because it provides a means for blessings to be transmitted through the one ministering to the one in need. "And Joshua, the son of Nun was filled with the spirit of wisdom, for Moses had laid his hands on him;" (Deuteronomy 34:9) The blessing of wisdom was given through Moses to Joshua by the laying on of hands.

There are other examples of blessings being given through the use of hands in prayer.

Then they began laying their hands on them, and they were receiving the Holy Spirit. (Acts 8:17)

And He (Jesus) could do no miracle there except that He laid His hands upon a few sick people and healed them. (Mark 6:5)

And at the hands of the apostles, many signs and wonders were taking place among the people. (Acts 5:12)

22 And they came to Bethsaida. And they brought a blind man to Him (Jesus), and entreated Him to touch him.
23 And taking the blind man by the hand, He brought him out of the village; and after spitting on his eyes, and laying His hands upon him, He asked him, "Do you see anything?"
24 And he looked up and said, "I see men, for I am seeing them like trees, walking about."
25 Then again, He laid His hands upon his eyes; and he looked intently and was restored, and began to see everything clearly. (Mark 8:22-25)

There are other references to the practice of laying on of hands: Acts 19:6, Matthew 8:15, Mark 7:32, 33, 35, Mark 5:22, 23, Acts 19:11, 12 and Acts 28:8, 9. Let the Scriptures convince you that the doctrine of laying on of hands is an elementary act for all believers, which allows God to transmit blessing from the one ministering to the one in need.

Jesus said, *"And these signs will accompany those who have believed...they will lay hands on the sick, and they will recover." (Mark 16:17, 18)* One characteristic of a Christian should be the laying on of hands for the good of another person. Become comfortable with laying your hands on your child as you pray for her during pregnancy. It is for her good.

As you lay hands on your child to pray, include requests for your child's (1) salvation and (2) development. Your child cannot pray for him or herself, so it is your responsibility to make sure your child receives the benefits of prayer.

<u>(1) Pray for your child's salvation.</u> In the previous chapter we discussed praying for the conception of your child's spirit. As the spirit develops during pregnancy, pray that your child will grow in sensitivity to godly things and in desire for a relationship with God.

The gospel of Luke lets us know that the prenatal child is sensitive and receptive to God. "But the angel said to him, 'Do not be afraid Zacharias, for your petition has been heard, and your wife Elizabeth will bear you a son, and you will give him the name John. And you will have joy and gladness, and many will rejoice at his birth. For he will be great in the sight of the Lord, and he will drink no wine or liquor; and he will be filled with the Holy Spirit while yet in his mother's womb.'" (Luke 1:13-15)

The spirit of John the Baptist could receive the presence of the Holy Spirit during the pregnancy period. Pray that your child's spirit would yearn for God's presence and the work of the Holy Spirit throughout his entire life.

Not only is the prenatal child sensitive and receptive to God, but also, he responds to God. Again, in the first chapter of Luke, verses 39-44, there is an example relating to John the Baptist. "Now, Mary arose and went with haste to the hill country, to a city of Judah, and entered the house of Zacharias and greeted Elizabeth. And it came about that when Elizabeth heard Mary's greeting the baby leaped in her womb; and Elizabeth was filled with the Holy Spirit. And she cried with a loud voice, and said, 'Blessed among women are you, and blessed is the fruit of your womb! And how has it happened to me, that the mother of my Lord should come to me? For behold, when the sound of your greeting reached my ears, the baby leaped in my womb for joy!'". John knew that the Savior was present and responded.

Because it is possible for your child to be sensitive and respond to God, even during pregnancy, pray that your child would begin to do so. Your prayers will be preparing your child for salvation by pointing his spirit, the only part of him that can truly worship, toward God. Praying that his spirit be made receptive to God is the primary way you should pray for his salvation.

The second way you should pray for your child is to ask God to prepare Christian people that your child will encounter during his life. Ask God to prepare them to speak and act in a way that will help secure your child's salvation. Most Christians can attribute their salvation experience, at least partially, to the influence of a friend, teacher, pastor, youth leader, evangelist, or another individual other than a parent. It is your responsibility to lead your children to the Lord, but pray that God will send others to be an influence that will complement your efforts.

(2) Pray for your child's development. Through the laying on of hands, pray for your child's physical and spiritual development. Her physical development is not as directly related to salvation as her spiritual development, but a proper physical development will provide order and normalcy in her life and give her the tools to receive the gospel (i.e. ears to hear the gospel and eyes to read the Bible).

Pray for each physical part before it develops. You can get a complete list through an obstetrician, but below are some of the development times.

Week 2 The embryonic disk is formed which will produce every organ and tissue in your baby's body.
Week 4 The heart and digestive tract take shape.
Week 5 Limb buds appear and the heart pumps blood.
Week 6 Eyes and ears begin to appear.
Week 7 Facial parts are complete including eyes, lips, tongue and nose.
Week 9 Sex is visually noticeable. Eyelids are formed.
Week 10 Bone cells form and movement begins.
Week 11 Organs assume their functions. Kidneys produce urine and the pancreas produces insulin.
Week 12 Lungs form. Breathing and swallowing motions take place.
Week 14 Nervous system begins to operate. Blood vessels develop.
Week 16 All organs and structures are formed and growth begins.
Week 22 Skeleton develops rapidly.
Week 27 A substance called surfactant forms in the lungs preparing them to function independently at birth.
Week 30 Under the skin, fat deposits form to insulate your baby against abrupt temperature change at birth.
Week 33 Antibodies are passed from mother to baby to protect him against disease until his own immune system takes over at 6 months.

Pray also for your baby's spiritual development. We have discussed the importance of praying for a spirit sensitive to and desiring God, but there are other parts of his spiritual development that warrant prayer.

Later in life, your child will be presented with many choices. He will have to decide whether or not to play with the knife he sees in the dishwasher or cross the busy street by herself. It will be her choice as to who she hangs out with, and she will determine if she will use or say no to alcohol and drugs.

Pray for a spirit of wisdom to be set flowing in her that will offer divine direction for tough decisions. Wisdom is a precious gift for all affairs of life, including accurately seeing Satan and hell compared to God and heaven. The apostle Paul, in 2 Corinthians 4:3, 4, says that people don't receive salvation because Satan has blinded them from the light of the gospel. A spirit of wisdom will allow your child to see the gospel as good news and the rejection of the gospel as bad news.

The book of Proverbs has much to say about the benefits of wisdom:

"How blessed is the man who finds wisdom, and the man who gains understanding. For its profit is better than the profit of silver, and its gain than fine gold. She is more precious than jewels; and nothing you desire compares with her. Long life is in her right hand; in her left hand are riches and honor. Her ways are pleasant ways, and all her paths are peace. She is a tree of life to those who take hold of her, and happy are all who hold her fast. The Lord by wisdom founded the earth; by understanding he established the heavens. By his knowledge the deeps were broken up, and the skies drop with dew. My son, let them not depart from your sight; keep sound wisdom and discretion, so they will be life to your soul, and adornment to your neck. Then you will walk in your way securely, and your foot will not stumble." (Proverbs 3:13-23)

"Acquire wisdom! Acquire understanding! Do not forget, nor turn away from the words of my mouth. Do not forsake her and she will guard you; love her and she will watch over you. The beginning of wisdom is: Acquire wisdom; and with all your acquiring, get understanding. Prize her, and she will exalt you; she will honor you if you embrace her. She will place on your head a garland of peace; she will present you with a crown of beauty." (Proverbs 4:5-9)

The benefits of wisdom are invaluable; life, riches, peace, happiness, security, safety, and honor. Pray daily for a spirit of wisdom to be active as part of your child's spiritual development. Pray especially that the presence of wisdom would prevent your child from being blinded to the gospel.

Pray, also, for a teachable spirit for your child. A teachable spirit will allow him to receive instruction that the stove is hot, the trash is off limits, and bugs are not food. More importantly it will cause understanding and acceptance of teaching from the Bible.

Being teachable prevents rebellion against instruction. When children get into trouble, it is because of defiance against guidance. When your child is old enough to receive instruction from the Bible, a teachable spirit will allow her to receive the benefits of accepting and following the Scriptures' direction. The direction of the Scriptures will lead her to a relationship with Jesus.

2. Read the Bible to Your Baby

Babies begin to hear during the twentieth week of pregnancy. Earlier we looked at John the Baptist in the womb, and we saw how his spirit responded to spiritual things. He also responded to sound. *"For behold, when the sound of your greeting reached my ears, the baby leaped in my womb for joy." (Luke 1:44)* When Mary said hello to Elizabeth, John heard also.

Because the unborn child can hear, it is important that he hear godly words. One way to let him hear godly words is to read the Bible to him. A home filled with godly words will provide an environment that is helpful to securing your child's salvation.

I have never read any literature discussing the effects of reading Scripture to an unborn baby, and, as far as I know, there is no concrete data proving that it is beneficial. However, there are several verses in the Bible that provide evidence that it is important to do so.

(1) In the account of John the Baptist, the Bible proves to us that babies can hear what is said; therefore, they can receive what is read to them. Studies show that a new born baby responds to her mother's voice because she has heard it while in the womb. Your baby will hear what you read to her from the Bible.

(2) I believe that the Word of God is powerful enough to benefit your child even though his mind cannot understand the meaning of the words. "For the Word of God is living and active and sharper than any two-edged sword, and piercing as far as the division of soul and spirit, of both joints and marrow, and able to judge the thoughts and intentions of the heart." (Hebrews 4:12)

The Scriptures you read your child can benefit your child because they are able to bypass the uncomprehending mind (soul) and speak directly to the spirit. I believe that the spirit of a prenatal child can receive and store God's Word even though the mind cannot yet understand.

When John the Baptist heard Mary's voice, he responded with joy. For him to respond with joy, there must have been an understanding of what was happening. John's mind did not understand what was spoken, but he understood that Mary and the unborn Jesus were in his hearing range. I believe that the words were heard and understood through his spirit.

Your unborn child will not understand the Bible with his mind, but he will benefit from what he hears because the Word of God can minister directly to his spirit.

(3) From looking at John, it appears that, when conception takes place and a spirit is born, the spirit is immediately functional. The spirit is not like the mind and body which require a long maturing process. John, while in the womb, could be filled with the Holy Spirit and understand what he heard through his spirit.

Since the spirit is functional in the womb, it can appraise God's Word as it is read. *"But a natural man does not accept the things of the Spirit of God; for they are foolishness to him, and he cannot understand them, because they are spiritually appraised." (1 Corinthians 2:14)* Even the mature mind is incapable of understanding the Bible because it is the spirit that receives the understanding. The spirit of your child, however, can benefit from hearing God's Word.

(4) Your child's spirit is fed by hearing the Bible. *"But He (Jesus) answered and said, 'It is written, "Man shall not live by bread alone, but on every word that proceeds out of the mouth of God."'" (Matthew 4:4)* Bread feeds the body and God's Word feeds the spirit.

In summary, it is important to read the Bible to your prenatal child because (1) Your child can hear it, (2) God's Word is able to minister directly to your child's spirit, (3) Your child's spirit can appraise God's Word, and (4) What your child hears will feed your child's spirit.

3. Portray an Attitude of Love, Not Strife

If we look, once again, at Luke 1:44, we can see that your prenatal child can experience emotion. *"For behold, when the sound of your greeting reached my ears, the baby leaped in my womb for joy."* The emotions to which your baby is subjected will impact him, so portray positive emotions.

Much has been written about bonding between parent and child after delivery. It is recommended that both parents have a significant amount of contact during the first hour after birth and regular contact during the hospital stay. The purpose of the bonding periods is an exchange of emotions, particularly love, between the parents and baby.

Marshall Klaus and John Kennell have conducted research regarding the area of exchange of love in bonding. A conventional control group was compared with a group participating in immediate and consistent subsequent bonding. The control group was allowed a brief look at the baby at birth, short contact after six hours and thirty minutes every four hours for feeding. Both groups were followed for up to five years. One month after birth, "bonding mothers" portrayed more of an attitude of love with more cuddling, comforting, and eye contact. At one year, the children cried less and were happier. Two years after birth, the mothers spoke to their children with more descriptive language and fewer commands. At five years of age, testing showed significantly higher language skills and IQs among the "bonding" children.

Research has also proven that bonding occurs before birth, as the baby's movements are felt and heartbeat is heard. The prenatal period is an opportunity for a strong bond to be created between parents and child. Portray an attitude of love toward your baby through your words and touching.

Tell her how excited you are to have her. Touch her and tell him how you look forward to holding her. Talk to her about how you are decorating her room because she is special. Explain to her how God loves her and wants her to grow up to be godly.

The object is to portray an attitude of love and to prevent an attitude of strife. James 3:16 in the King James Version says, *"For where envying and strife is, there is confusion and every evil work."* If an attitude of strife is permitted, then the door is swung wide open for the entrance of evil.

If pregnancy causes you nausea, fatigue, discomfort, lost sleep and inconvenience, make sure that you do not portray resentment and anger toward your child. Resentment and anger are strife and are followed by "every evil work". Instead, tell your baby that you love him and will happily endure anything to bring him into the world.

"Love is patient, love is kind, and is not jealous; love does not brag and is not arrogant, does not act unbecomingly; it does

not seek its own, is not provoked, does not take into account a wrong suffered, does not rejoice in unrighteousness, but rejoices with the truth; bears all things, believes all things, hopes all things, endures all things. Love never fails..." (1 Corinthians 13:4-8)

Love never fails and strife brings every evil work. The choice is yours. Choose to portray an attitude of love not strife.

4. Provide an Environment of Peace and Honor of God

Closely related to portraying an attitude of love is providing an environment of peace and honor of God. Anytime that love locks out strife, there will be a tendency toward peace and honor in the home, but there are other things to keep in line that promote a proper environment for your baby's development before birth. Be selective with television, music, and conversation so they are kept in line with godly values.

Television is an amazing invention. Because I am electronically ignorant, I marvel how people in a studio can be captured as electrical impulses. Those impulses are sent hundreds of miles and decoded as a picture on my TV. The capability that TV offers to God's kingdom is massive. One broadcast can share the gospel with billions of people.

The shows you select to watch will partially determine if your home will have an environment of peace and honor of God. Christian and family programming will help create the atmosphere that you want for your child during the prenatal months and following.

Because your baby can hear in the womb and is sensitive to what goes on around him, select your shows with care. Choose the programs that fall in line with your Christian values. Do not subject your child to shows, now, that you would not want him to watch when older. Select godly and peaceful shows.

As a parent you are interested in keeping the influence of Satan out of your home. If he knocked on your front door, you certainly would not let him in. You would realize that he was not there for your good, and you would close the door in his face.

John 10:10 describes Satan and his mission. *"The thief comes only to steal and kill and destroy."* Because you would stop Satan at your front door, he chooses other means to enter your home. TV is one of his favorite choices. If you would not give him even a crack at the front door, then do not open your entire house to him through the TV. He comes in with murder, violence, foul language, lust, greed, materialism, adultery, and theft. If you are to be successful in providing your baby an environment of peace and honor of God, you must be selective in what you watch.

1 Corinthians 6:9-11 tells you the kind of things that do not belong in your home. Do not watch shows that promote or wash over these sins. "Or do you not know that the unrighteous shall not inherit the kingdom of God? Do not be deceived; neither fornicators nor idolaters, nor adulterers, nor effeminate, nor homosexuals, nor thieves, nor the covetous, nor drunkards, nor revilers, nor swindlers, shall inherit the kingdom of God. And such were some of you; but you were washed, but you were sanctified, but you were justified in the name of the Lord Jesus Christ, and in the Spirit of our God."

Choose shows that are wholesome and family or Christian oriented. Bar Satan from entering your home through shows that have ungodly material. Provide for your baby an environment of peace and honor of God by keeping your television viewing in line.

Music is another area, to be kept in line, that helps determine your home atmosphere. Again, it is your choice what you allow in your home. Music can cause peace or stir up things. It can have a beneficial or harmful message. It can honor or be shameful to God.

Music, like TV, is one of Satan's favorite choices for gaining a foothold in your home. However, he can have an influence through music only if you permit him. Use music to fill your mind with good and not evil. "Finally, brethren, whatever is true, whatever is honorable, whatever is right, whatever is pure, whatever is lovely, whatever is of good repute, if there is any excellence and if anything worthy of praise, let your mind dwell on these things." (Philippians 4:8)

Listening to wholesome music can not only help keep Satan's influence out of your home, but also it can also help drive him out, if the music is godly. In the Old Testament, King Saul had a problem with Satan tormenting him through an evil spirit. David used music to drive the evil spirit away. *"So it came about whenever the evil spirit came to Saul, David would take the harp and play it with his hand; and Saul would be refreshed and be well, and the evil spirit would depart from him." (1 Samuel 16:23)*

Make music work for you to provide an environment of peace and honor of God for your baby. Avoid music that has a worldly message so that Satan's influence is not invited into your home. Choose a beat that is soothing. Keep your use of music in line.

Another area to keep consistent with godly values is the conversation that takes place in your home. Your prenatal child is subjected to the words that are spoken around him, and, I believe, we grossly underestimate the impact that words can have. I have seen faces droop because someone has said, "You look tired today". Tears flow because of an insensitive comment, and confidence can be destroyed because of the words, "You will never amount to anything".

Words are very powerful, and Proverbs 18:21 states that as well as it can be stated. *"Death and life are in the power of the tongue and those who love it will eat its fruit."* Your home conversation can cause your family to flourish or die and can set your baby on a path toward God or the world.

Guard your conversation so that the fruit that is produced from the words in your home is sweet and not bitter. Choose words that bring life by talking about God, His blessings upon you, the good qualities of people, the nice weather, what you liked about the sermon, what the Bible says about a life issue, and other positive subjects. Positive conversations are productive while the absence of talk about God and the presence of gossip, complaining, and critical words are destructive.

God is listening to our conversations. The words spoken in our homes are so important to Him that He judges each one. "And I say to you, that every careless word that men shall speak, they shall render account for it in the day of judgment." (Matthew 12:36)

Scripture is very plain in teaching that some conversation is improper in our homes. "...They go around from house to house; and not merely idle, but also gossips and busy bodies, talking about things not proper to mention." (1 Timothy 5:13) "Let no unwholesome word proceed from your mouth, but only such a word as is good for edification according to the need of the moment, that it may give grace to those who hear." (Ephesians 4:29)

Your home is no place for any kind of unwholesome or negative conversation. Only allow conversation that would enlighten or encourage your prenatal child and other listeners. It is your privilege to control the conversations in your home. It is, also, your responsibility.

God wants our conversations to be ones to which He is proud to attach His Son's name. *"And whatever you do in word or deed, do all in the name of the Lord Jesus."* (Colossians 3:17) If you would feel uncomfortable with Jesus in the conversation, do not have the conversation. Do not cause your child to hear words you do not want God to hear.

The tongue must be watched carefully and diligently because it can benefit or harm the speaker and hearer. *"But avoid worldly and empty chatter, for it will lead to further ungodliness." (2 Timothy 2:16)* Gossip, as an example, is not only wrong itself, but it leads to further ungodliness in the form of strife toward the one being discussed. The speaker and listener are harmed. Your unborn child is subject to the harm, and if the home environment is not changed, he will grow up learning that the sin of gossip is acceptable.

Do not allow your conversation to train your child to stumble because of the words he will one day speak. Instead, teach him, even now, to choose wholesome and godly words. "It would be better for him if a millstone were hung around his neck and he were thrown into the sea, than that he should cause one of these little ones to stumble." (Luke 17:2)

The tongue is difficult to control, but it must be disciplined because its product, words, impact the course of your baby's life, her relationship with God, and her eternal destiny. The third chapter of James discusses the difficulty of taming the tongue and the tongue's impact on the course of your child's life.

2 For we all stumble in many ways. If any one does not stumble in what he says, he is a perfect man, able to bridle the whole body as well.

3 Now if we put bits into the horses' mouths so that they may obey us, we direct their entire body as well.

4 Behold, the ships also, though they are great and are driven by strong winds, are still directed by a small rudder, wherever the inclination of the pilot desires.

5 So also the tongue is a small part of the body, and yet it boasts of great things. Behold how great a forest is set aflame by such a small fire!

6 And the tongue is a fire, the very world of iniquity; the tongue is set among our members as that which defiles the entire body, and sets on fire the course of our life, and is set on fire by hell.

7 For every species of beasts and birds, of reptiles and creatures of the sea, is tamed and has been tamed by the human race.

8 But no one can tame the tongue; it is a restless evil and full of deadly poison.

9 With it we bless our Lord and Father; and with it we curse men, who have been made in the likeness of God;

10 from the same mouth come both blessing and cursing. My brethren, these things ought not to be this way.

11 Does a fountain send out from the same opening both fresh and bitter water?" (James 3:2-11)

The tongue is very difficult to tame because Satan realizes the impact of words and works hard to set your words ablaze with anger, hate, revenge, and filth. Even though no one can tame the tongue by his own efforts, *"... the things impossible with men are possible with God." (Luke 18:27)* It is important to rise to the challenge of controlling your words.

The reason it is important is that the tongue impacts the course of your child's life. If left untamed, the tongue will be "set on fire by hell" and then "set on fire the course of" your child's life. The burning fire of rejection can be felt by your child because of words like, "I wish we had stopped after two kids." Conversely, your child can experience love and peace because he hears, "You are special. God was good to give you to us." The words you choose make the difference.

The tongue should produce favorable words all the time and not a mixture of bad with the good. James says it is improper to bless God and curse man. The tongue should always produce words of blessing. James, also, says that only clean and pure words should be spoken, like the fountain that always puts out clean and pure water.

When my church erected a building, we installed water fountains. Once in service, we expected those fountains to always produce fresh water. The fountains were useful and a source of refreshment to us until dirt got into the water line. As long as dirt was mixed with fresh water, the fountains were kept out of service because of the harm they could cause.

God expects your tongue to always produce refreshing words for the benefit of others. Your words can keep you out of service in God's kingdom. He wants to pour His power through a fountain that will produce pure refreshing results. Your unborn child hears the conversation in your home. Choose refreshing words, the kind God will empower.

There are many Scriptures that teach the power, importance, and results of conversation. Below are a few.

"For by your words you shall be justified and by your words you shall be condemned." (Matthew 12:37)

"Truly I say to you, whoever says to this mountain, 'Be taken up and cast into the sea', and does not doubt in his heart, but

believes that what he says in going to happen, it shall be granted him." (Mark 11:23)

There is one who speaks like the thrusts of a sword, but the tongue of the wise brings healing. (Proverbs 12:18)

He who guards his mouth and his tongue, guards his soul from trouble. (Proverbs 21:23)

9 That if you confess with your mouth Jesus as Lord, and believe in your heart that God raised Him from the dead, you shall be saved; 10 for with the heart man believes, resulting in righteousness, and with the mouth he confesses, resulting in salvation." (Romans 10:9, 10)

Your conversation will affect your prenatal child so guard your words. Speak words that you would want your child to hear if he could fully understand the English language. Speak words that you would not be ashamed for God to hear.

Tame your tongue, and do not let it be set on fire by hell. Be selective in choosing TV shows and music that fall in line with your Christian values. Television, music, and conversation should all be kept in line so that an environment of peace and honor of God is provided for your child.

There are many Scriptures that reveal that peacefulness is very much related to Christianity. Your responsibility is to introduce your child to a lifestyle that God wants for His people. One way you can accomplish that is to provide peace in your home.

We have already seen that God's wisdom is related to peace. *"But wisdom from above is first pure, then peaceable..." (James 3:17)* Let's look at other Scriptures that prove that peace is something that is characteristic of God and His people. Allow these Scriptures to convince you that a peaceful home resembles the character of God and shows your child how God wants His people to live.

Jesus' character is one of peace
For a child will be born to us, a son will be given to us; and the government will rest on His shoulders; and His name will be called Wonderful Counselor, Mighty God, Eternal Father, Prince of Peace. (Isaiah 9:6)

Now may the Lord of peace Himself continually grant you peace in every circumstance... (2 Thessalonians 3:16)

God's character is one of peace
The things you have learned and received and heard and seen in me, practice these things; and the God of peace shall be with you. (Philippians 4:9)

The Holy Spirit's character is one of peace
22 But the fruit of the Spirit is love, joy, peace, patience, kindness, goodness, faithfulness,
23 gentleness, self-control; against such things there is no law. (Galatians 5:22, 23)
        The character of each member of the Trinity includes the attribute of peace. A peaceful home resembles that godly character.

Peace is a blessing
The Lord will give strength to His people; the Lord will bless His people with peace. (Psalm 29:11)

God blesses those who make peace
Blessed are the peacemakers, for they shall be called sons of God. (Matthew 5:9)

Trusting God produces peace
The steadfast of mind Thou wilt keep in perfect peace, because he trusts in Thee. (Isaiah 26:3)

Obeying God produces peace
Those who love Thy law have great peace, and nothing causes them to stumble. (Psalm 119:165)

1 My son do not forget my teaching, but let your heart keep my commandments;
2 For length of days and years of life, and peace they will add to you. (Proverbs 3:1, 2)

        Peace is characteristic of God and His people. A peaceful home resembles the character of God and shows your child how God wants His people to live. Establish peace now because your prenatal child is sensitive to his environment.

5. Walk in Faith Concerning Your Child's Health and Your Pregnancy

Walking in faith is related to securing your prenatal child's salvation. It subjects him to the correct Christian response in uncertain situations. It develops in you a method to approach many later situations, where you will have an opportunity to set an example for him. Walking in faith shows him what it is like to live like God wants him to live.

Remember, everything we will discuss in this book involves preparing you, your child, and his environment for the purpose of leading your child to Jesus. Walking in faith during the pregnancy prepares you to walk in faith as your child grows up. Your example of walking by faith will one day teach your child to respond to uncertain circumstances in the manner he has seen you respond. Walking by faith also provides a positive rather than fearful environment for him. Your example of walking by faith is a prenatal activity that will provide a foundation for your child to respond to God and walk in faith himself when he is old enough to make that decision.

With the huge increase in malpractice law suits, obstetricians have become extremely cautious. Some have even stopped practicing obstetrics and limited themselves to gynecology. This prevailing attitude caused my wife's obstetrician to consider everything that could possibly be wrong with our son during pregnancy.

The battle was to prevent the doctor's concern for our welfare from producing fear in our minds. After all, tests are only run when there might be something wrong. The correct Christian response is not to be fearful of the way things appear and move on knowing that God is in control.2 Corinthians 5:7 says, *"For we walk by faith, not by sight."*

Before proceeding, it is important to note that we liked our obstetrician very much, felt that he was an excellent doctor and would have placed ourselves under his care again if needed. He was very conscientious and considered all alternatives with our care in mind.

Let's look at an example where we had the chance to choose between faith and fear. Sometime around the fourth month it "appeared" that we had major problems. My wife's size had not increased enough, and the baby's heartbeat could not be found. This was our first opportunity to walk by faith and not by the way things appeared.

An ultrasound test was scheduled for a few days later. During those few days before the test, the correct response was to look past appearances and see God in control. We had to take captive the thoughts and speculations of the mind.

"For though we walk in the flesh, we do not war according to the flesh, for the weapons of our warfare are not of the flesh but divinely powerful for the destruction of fortresses. We are destroying speculations and every lofty thing raised up against the knowledge of God, and taking every thought captive to the obedience of Christ." (2 Corinthians 10:3-5)

The mind is trained, by the world, to speculate that the baby is probably very sick or even dead, but those thoughts must be taken captive. If the thoughts were left to run rampant, worry, sorrow, and mental anguish would have resulted because of choosing to believe what we speculated to be true.

If we had warred according to the flesh, we would have walked believing only what we saw, but we fought with the divine weapon of walking by faith. We trusted God to be in control even though what we saw was contradictory. We trusted Him to produce a healthy baby even though the evidence was in opposition.

Speculations were destroyed by refusing to dwell on appearances. Thoughts were taken captive by remembering God was at work. We walked in faith concerning our baby's health. We refused to walk by sight.

The day for the test arrived, and the ultrasound equipment was turned on. There on the monitor was a tiny pulsating heart, and a healthy baby turned in a position that would make a heartbeat difficult to detect with an external amplifying device.

God had been in control. Our son was healthy the whole time even though circumstances looked unfavorable. God was producing a small baby so that he could be delivered naturally. The breaks in my wife's pelvis, from the auto accident mentioned earlier, would have caused a larger baby to be born by cesarean section.

Smallness, by sight, could have been interpreted as unhealthiness, but God was purposely causing smallness for our good. We practiced, and subjected our baby to, the right response. We walked by faith and not by sight.

Abraham in the Old Testament faced situations requiring him to walk by faith that can teach you how to respond in situations requiring faith. He looked at the appearance of his circumstances but believed God to make the outcome different.

"And without becoming weak in faith he contemplated his own body, now as good as dead since he was about a hundred years old, and the deadness of Sarah's womb; yet, with respect to the promise of God, he did not waver in unbelief, but grew strong in faith, giving glory to God, and being fully assured that what He had promised, He was able also to perform." (Romans 4:19-21)

God promised Abraham that he would have many descendants even though, at one hundred years old, he had no children because his wife was barren. By sight, it was impossible due to his age and her infertility. By faith, Abraham trusted God to perform His promise. The promise was fulfilled and Isaac was born. If God has promised something, you can walk by faith knowing it will come to pass no matter how the circumstances look.

John's gospel records the following. *"Martha therefore said to Jesus, 'Lord, if you had been here, my brother would not have died. Even now I know that whatever you ask of God, God will give you'. Jesus said to her, 'Your brother shall rise again'. And when He had said these things, He cried out with a loud voice, 'Lazarus, come forth'. He who died came forth, bound hand and foot with wrappings; and his face was wrapped around with a cloth. Jesus said to them, 'Unbind him, and let him go'". (John 11:21-23, 43-44)*

Circumstances cannot look worse than being dead four days. By then, decay has begun and the body deteriorates. No matter what sight tells us, if God says something, it will come to pass. Lazarus was dead, but Jesus said he would live. Abraham and Sarah were incapable of having children, but God said they would have a son. Walk by faith and do not be defeated by what you see.

The second situation Abraham faced that can teach you how to respond in situations requiring faith involved Isaac. God promised Abraham he would have a son and Isaac was born. He, also, promised to make Abraham's descendants as numerous as the stars which would require Isaac to have children and grandchildren and so forth.

Isaac was necessary to fulfill God's promise of countless descendants. With that in mind, God asked Abraham to do a peculiar thing.

1 Now it came about after these things that God tested Abraham, and said to him, "Abraham!"
2 And he said, "Here I am." And He said, "Take now your son, your only son, whom you love, Isaac, and go to the land of Moriah; and

offer him there as a burnt offering on one of the mountains of which I will tell you."
3 So Abraham rose early in the morning and saddled his donkey, and took two of his young men with him and Isaac his son; and he split wood for the burnt offering, and arose and went to the place God had told him. (Genesis 22:1-3)

If Abraham had chosen to walk by sight, he would have envisioned his only son burning on the altar. He would have seen those countless descendants as nothing more than a dream. He probably would have questioned if he really had heard God.

The Scriptures are clear that Abraham kept on walking by faith. Let's continue with Genesis 22:5. *"And Abraham said to his young men, 'Stay here with the donkey, and I and the lad will go yonder; and we will worship and return to you'."* Abraham planned on returning with Isaac even though the circumstances looked adverse.

In verses 7 and 8, we see more evidence of Abraham's faith.

7 And Isaac spoke to Abraham his father and said, "My father!" and he said, "Here I am my son". And he said, "Behold the fire and the wood, but where is the lamb for the burnt offering?"
8 And Abraham said, "God will provide for Himself the lamb for the burnt offering my son." So the two of them walked on together.

Abraham knew God would do something that would allow Isaac to produce millions of descendants. He supposed God would provide a lamb as a substitute.

As the ceremony progressed there was no substitute for Isaac. It looked like Abraham would have to slay his only son. Look at verses 9 and 10.

9 Then they came to the place of which God had told them; and Abraham built the altar there, and arranged the wood, and bound his son Isaac, and laid him on the altar on top of the wood.
10 And Abraham stretched out his hand, and took the knife to slay his son.

Even now, Abraham is walking by faith, convinced that God will remain true to His promise. I can hear him talking to himself, "I thought, surely, God would send a lamb. I wonder how

He will keep His promise. Whatever method He chooses, God will come through even if He has to raise Isaac from the dead."

Hebrews 11:17-19 lets us know what Abraham was thinking as he prepared to raise the knife.

17 By faith Abraham, when he was tested, offered up Isaac; and he who had received the promises was offering up his only begotten son;
18 It was he to whom it was said, "In Isaac your descendants shall be called."
19 He considered that God is able to raise men even from the dead; from which he also received him back as a type.

Let's go back to Genesis 22. The knife was in the air, and in Abraham's mind the sacrifice was complete. However, Abraham was walking by faith, knowing God would raise Isaac from the dead to fulfill the promise. Just before the knife started down, God intervened.

11 But the angel of the Lord called to him from heaven and said, "Abraham, Abraham!" And he said, "Here I am."
12 And he said, "Do not stretch out your hand against the lad, and do nothing to him; for now I know that you fear God, since you have not withheld your son, your only son from Me."
13 Then Abraham raised his eyes and looked, and behold, behind him a ram caught in the thicket by his horns; and Abraham went and took the ram and offered him up for a burnt offering in the place of his son.
14 And Abraham called the name of that place The Lord Will Provide, as it is said to this day, "In the mount of the Lord it will be provided." (Genesis 22:11-14)

Abraham's example teaches you to take a realistic look at the appearance of the circumstances, but believe God to make the outcome different. He shows you how to face uncertain situations and live the way God wants his people to live. It was to Abraham's advantage to walk by faith and not by sight.

It is advantageous for you to walk by faith concerning your child's health and your pregnancy. Events can be uncertain. Walking by faith during this time will prepare you to walk by faith during uncertain times once your child is born. Trust God for the outcome no matter how circumstances appear.

Just as Abraham's faith is an example to you, your faith will be an example to your child. He will see how God wants him to live and learn to put his faith in a God that intervenes on his behalf. Learn to walk by faith during pregnancy so that you can show and instruct your child how to walk by faith when he is old enough.

6. Prepare Yourself to Take Care of Your Baby's Needs

Your baby will be totally dependent on you for everything. The purpose of being prepared to care for her is to prevent her living in an environment of frustration. There are enough other opportunities for frustration, other than not being prepared to care for her.

There will be lost sleep, inopportune crying, untimely messes, and reduced church and social activities. These can lead to frustration. Do not add more opportunity for frustration by being unprepared to meet your baby's needs.

I believe that a peaceful home environment is very helpful in securing your child's salvation. Peace is characteristic of the things of God and the Christian life. Growing up surrounded by peacefulness reveals the character of God and how He wants His children to live. Peace shelters your child from the negative impact of strife and frustration. Prepare yourself to take care of your baby's needs because your readiness will help you keep peace in your home.

When the time for our son's birth came, my wife and I were well prepared for the delivery. We had attended natural childbirth classes, studied the literature, and practiced the techniques. Our readiness allowed us to exercise control over the labor and delivery process. The birth was a great success, totally without frustration, painful yet peaceful.

Caring for our son's needs, once born, was a different story. I had only held one or two babies. I changed a diaper for the first time in the hospital. I had never fed, clothed, or bathed a baby. My preparation was almost nonexistent. I was incapable of caring for his needs without significant frustration.

Through on the job training and the advice of experienced parents, I learned how to care for my son's needs. Diapers became routine, holding him became natural, bath time became fun, and frustration went away.

I wish I had prepared during the prenatal months because I could have prevented my son from being subject to an environment that sometimes was characterized by frustration. Had I been ready, there would have been many opportunities to show him control and peace instead of uncertainty and frustration. Be prepared to care for your baby to help keep peace in your home.

SUMMARY

The process of securing your child's salvation should begin before conception and continue through the prenatal months.

1. Lay hands on your child and pray for his physical and spiritual development.
2. Read the Bible to your child; God's Word ministers to all ages.
3. Lock out Satan by portraying an attitude of love not strife.
4. Provide an environment of peace and honor of God by carefully selecting the television shows, music, and conversation that is permitted in your home.
5. Practice showing your child how God wants his children to live by walking in faith concerning your child's health and your pregnancy.
6. Provide peace and prevent frustration by being prepared to care for your baby's needs before he arrives.

Sure, you may have to sacrifice or change habits, but your efforts are building a foundation that will point your child toward salvation. Keep a vision of your child coming to Jesus through your efforts. Proverbs 29:18 in the King James Version says, *"Where there is no vision the people perish..."* Sometimes parent's children perish because the parents had no vision for their children's salvation.

Possibly, the most important endeavor you will ever undertake is to be part of securing your child's salvation. Be prepared to succeed before your child arrives.

POSTPARTUM ACTIVITIES (FOLLOWING BIRTH)

We have looked at several activities that prepare you, your home, and your child before the event of his birth.

Preconception
1. Experience salvation yourself
2. Put your spiritual life in order
3. Build your faith on God's Word
4. Pray for wisdom
5. Learn to hear from God
6. Be financially ready
7. Pray for your child's physical conception
8. Pray for your child's spiritual conception

Prenatal
1. Lay hands on your baby and pray
2. Read the Bible to your baby
3. Portray an attitude of love not strife
4. Provide an environment of peace and honor of God
5. Walk in faith concerning your child's health and your pregnancy
6. Prepare yourself to take care of your baby's needs

Before your child's birth you are unable to see the baby for whom you have been diligently performing these activities. When you see her and hold her, you will know your efforts have been worth the perseverance and sacrifice. Your love for her will cause you to want the best for her and that is what you have been doing through the preconception and prenatal activities.

If your baby is already born or has developed into a toddler, preschooler, or even teenager, do not panic over the fact that you are late in getting started. Ideally, you should have started before conception and continued through pregnancy, but it is not too late. Today, begin building into your life and home the foundation that equips you to secure your child's salvation.

Dr. James Dobson, Past President of Focus on the Family, a nonprofit organization committed to the preservation of the family, believes that the fifth year is the most crucial in securing a child's salvation. Around the age of five a child reaches a decision point. He either begins to accept his parents' religious ideas as his own or begins to question them and reject them. What he has been taught during those years forms the basis for his decision.

My ideas fall in line with Dr. Dobson's. The process of securing your child's salvation begins before conception. By first grade a solid foundation should be formed. Upon this strong foundation he can make the correct decision concerning Jesus. The Catholic Church says, "Give me a child until he is seven and he will be a Catholic forever". Proverbs 22:6 says, *"Train up a child in the way he should go. Even when he is old he will not depart from it."*

Sometimes it is easy to dismiss the ideas of an author or a church denomination, but when God's Word (Proverbs 22:6) confirms the fact that childhood training is essential, it should not be ignored. Take advantage of the preschool years, and instill in your child values she will likely hold onto forever. Train her in principles from which you do not want her to depart when she is older.

Before training can take place, there must be a plan of attack. A runner has a schedule of jogging, stretching, sprinting, and practicing techniques. A new military recruit undergoes marching, conditioning, discipline, and teaching concerning weaponry and war strategy. The drill sergeant has a definite plan upon the recruit's arrival.

The purpose of this chapter is to help you establish a plan for training your child in such a way as to direct him toward God and godly values. The object is to train him in the way God wants him to go, so that when he is older he will choose to live by what he has been taught.

As a little boy, I developed a passion for baseball, and my father taught me the necessary skills; to throw, to catch, and to hit. He taught me to throw with my right hand and catch with my left, and he taught me to bat right handed. To this day I have not departed from his teaching.

My father had a choice. Some baseball players throw right handed and some left. The same holds true for catching and hitting. He could have taught me the way that he did, the complete opposite, or left me alone to learn for myself. The point is that my entire experience with baseball was directed by my father's training.

At one time I flirted with batting left handed but it felt unnatural, and I came back to right handed. What I was taught as a little boy, I chose not to depart from as an adult.

The same principles apply in spiritual training of a child. He can be trained to go the way of the cross, the way of the world, or left alone to choose a way for himself. The Bible teaches that the way he goes as a child will probably be the way he will go as an adult. It is your responsibility to show him the way to the cross. He may flirt with other ideas, but chances are that he will come back to what you taught him.

As you proceed with your child's spiritual training, continue to utilize the appropriate preconception and prenatal activities. You should keep yourself, your finances, and your home environment in shape all the time. The need for these does not pass away at your child's birth.

Training is a dedicated process that calls for daily implementation of a definite plan. Each year, around the first of March, hundreds of baseball players report to Spring Training in Florida and Arizona. Spring Training is not a time when you practice if you feel like it. Each day has a specific schedule for the morning and the afternoon.

Experienced coaches lead the athletes through planned activities designed to teach needed skills. The players are watched carefully to see how they are progressing, and if they need additional help in a weak area, extra guidance is provided where needed.

The coaches are there because they know what it takes to be a baseball player. Their objective is to direct the players toward a target of perfection. They watch each player and build skills that will help him reach the target.

You, as a parent, are a coach and your home is the playing field. Your objective should be to direct your child toward God and to a target lifestyle of perfection. Watch his progress carefully and build principles into his life that will help him reach the target.

God wants his children to aim for perfection. *"Therefore, you are to be perfect, as your heavenly Father is perfect."* *(Matthew 5:48)* He, also, wants Christians to be the coaches that direct the immature toward perfection. Ephesians 4:11, 12 in the King James Version says, *"And He gave some, apostles; and some, prophets; and some evangelists, and some pastors and teachers; for the perfecting of the saints, for the work of the ministry, for the edifying of the body of Christ:"* It is your responsibility to direct your child toward salvation and then toward perfection with the help of others.

Begin coaching from birth to take advantage of the first five impressionable years. A child should not be left alone to form his own ideas about God because the chances are high that the ideas will be incorrect. By guiding him into accurate spiritual training, you are forming the foundation upon which he will form his own concept of God. Spiritual training is not cramming God down his throat; it provides the basis for his own decisions. The purpose of spiritual training is to teach him truthful information so that he can make an enlightened decision for himself.

When a baby goose is born, he becomes attached to the first moving object he sees. Usually that is his mother, but the baby goose knows no difference if the moving object is something else. The gosling will follow the first thing he sees, which could be a mother duck, a person, or an object pulled by a string. The early period of his life is the key to what he will follow the rest of his life.

Similarly, a child becomes attached to ideas that are brought before him during the early period of his life. The first five years are vital in determining what he will follow the rest of his life. If you teach and live correct spiritual truths before your child, it is likely that he will follow them forever.

Your words and your life will broadcast spiritual truths to your child. Your broadcast occurs anytime your child observes you, not just when you have a formal teaching time. In everything you do with or around your child, have the intention of showing him something about God.

Deuteronomy 6:6-9 reads, "And these words, which I am commanding you today, shall be on your heart; and you shall teach them diligently to your sons and shall talk of them when you sit in your house and when you walk by the way and when you lie down and when you rise up. And you shall bind them as a sign on your hand and they shall be as frontal on your forehead. And you shall write them on the doorposts of your house and on your gates."

Notice how encompassing this command is. Teach God's Word inside your house and outside your house. Instruct your child when resting and during activity. Hang plaques in your house that display spiritual truths. The passing of godly values to your child is not a weekly tutoring session but a lifestyle. It is a sunrise to sunset responsibility.

Psychologists have confirmed that a child forms a picture of God in his mind based on his experiences with his parents. When his parents truly love him, he sees God as a loving God. When he submits to their authority, he is learning to submit to God's authority.

Your responsibility is to broadcast, through your lifestyle, a picture of God that is representative of His true nature. The two most important characteristics of God's nature that you can live before your children are unconditional love and merciful authority. Your child should know that there are no conditions attached to earning your love. The fact that he is your child is enough. He should also know that he is under your authority. He should understand that you deal with him mercifully for his benefit.

Part of your plan to direct your child toward God and godly values is to show your child the character of God through your unconditional love for him and your merciful authority toward him.

Let us look at other concepts your plan should address. With the permission of Dr. James Dobson, I will be using many of his ideas throughout the rest of the chapter. The ideas come from his book Dr. Dobson Answers Your Questions About Raising Children.

Your child should be taught the following scriptural concepts. They are crucial in directing her toward securing her salvation.

Concept 1. Love God with All Her Heart
Concept 2. Follow God's Will
Concept 3. Keep God's Commandments
Concept 4. Love Others as Herself
Concept 5. Practice the Fruit of the Spirit
Concept 6. Practice Proper Stewardship

Concept 1. Love God with All Her Heart

28 And one of the scribes came and heard them arguing, and recognizing that He had answered them well, asked Him, "What commandment is the foremost of all?"
29 Jesus answered, "The foremost is, 'Hear O Israel; The Lord our God is one Lord;
30 and you shall love the Lord your God with all your heart, and with all your soul, and with all your mind, and with all your strength.'" (Mark 12:28-30)

The most important thing you can teach your child is to love God unlimitedly and to put God first in everything she does. When you love someone strongly, that love motivates you to all kinds of proper actions.

Your child will learn to love God according to the measure of love you show toward her and toward God. The way she is loved, she will learn to love. If the love is sporadic, she will learn to express love to God when she feels like it. If she is loved only when she accomplishes something splendid, she will learn to love God when God performs a miracle. But, if she is loved consistently, tenderly unconditionally, and mercifully out of the abundance of your heart, she will learn to love God (and you) with her whole heart.

In addition to being taught by your love for her, she will be taught by observing your display of love toward God. The measure of love you offer to God will help determine whether she loves God partially or with all her heart, soul, mind, and strength. Teach her to love God by expressing your love to her and to God.

Is She Learning about God's Love?

There are several things your child should know about God's love. We have already seen that God's love is unconditional. He loves us whether or not we deserve it.

1 John 4:19 lets us know that God loved us even though we did not love Him. *"We love, because He first loved us."*

He loved us first even though we were filthy in sin. "But God demonstrates His own love toward us, in that while we were yet sinners, Christ died for us." (Romans 5:8)

Nothing can come between God's love and His children. "For I am convinced that neither death, nor life, nor angels, nor principalities, nor things present, nor things to come, nor powers, nor height, nor depth, nor any other created thing shall be able to separate us from the love of God, which is in Christ Jesus our Lord." (Romans 8:38, 39)

God's love is unselfish. The Greek word used when talking about God's love is agape. Its meaning includes sacrifice and giving. The God kind of love is unselfish.

God's love takes action. Because He loves us, He acts on our behalf. God's greatest love inspired action was accomplished when He sent Jesus to the cross for us. *"For God so loved the world, that He gave His only begotten Son, that whoever believes in Him shall not perish, but have eternal life." (John 3:16)* God's love is not dormant or dead; God's love takes action.

Another attribute of God's love is that it is eternal. Jeremiah 31:3 says, "I have loved you with an everlasting love; therefore, I have drawn you with loving kindness."

1. God's love is unconditional.
2. He loved us first even though we did not love Him.
3. He loved even though we were sinners.
4. Nothing can separate God's children from His love.
5. God's love is unselfish and sacrificial.

6. God's love takes action for our good.
7. God's love is eternal.

Teach your child these attributes of God's love and read her stories from the Bible that show how God expressed His care for His people.

The Bible is full of accounts that relate God's care for His people. Each can allow your child to learn something about God's love. A few examples follow below.

God selected Israel as his people, and when Pharaoh put them in slavery, God set them free because He loved them. God's love causes Him to deliver us from trying circumstances.

6 For you are a holy people to the Lord your God; the Lord your God has chosen you to be a people for His own possession out of all the peoples who are on the face of the earth.
7 The Lord did not set His love on you nor choose you because you were more in number than any of the peoples, for you were the fewest of all peoples,
8 but because the Lord loved you and kept the oath which He swore to your forefathers, the Lord brought you out by a mighty hand, and redeemed you from the house of slavery, from the hand of Pharaoh King of Egypt. (Deuteronomy 7:6-8)

Later in Deuteronomy, there is another account that reveals God's love for His people. It shows us another way God's love takes action. Not only does God's love provide escape from the midst of difficult situations, but also it turns those situations into blessings. *"Nevertheless, the Lord your God was not willing to listen to Balaam, but the Lord your God turned the curse into a blessing for you because the Lord your God loves you."* *(Deuteronomy 23:5)*

Because of God's love, Noah was saved from the flood. Daniel was protected from the lions. David was able to slay Goliath. Abraham was given Isaac. Lepers were made clean. Thousands were fed. Lazarus was raised from the dead. More importantly, however, because of God's love, Jesus' blood was shed, and He died for your child. *"To Him who loved us, and released us from our sins by His blood." (Revelation 1:5)*

There is no better statement of God's love, to your child, than the fact that Jesus gave Himself to die in your child's place. Help him learn about God's love.

Is She Learning the Beauty of Jesus' Birth and Death?

Learning the real Christmas and Easter stories can develop your child's love for God. You should tell her about God's great love for her that resulted in Jesus being born as a Christmas gift especially for her. Your child should learn that Jesus died for her because it was the only way God could be her friend forever.

Jesus' birth and death are beautiful stories that show how much God loves your child. Help her understand God's love for her in these two gospel stories.

Is She Learning to Read the Bible?

Getting to know someone causes our love for that person to deepen. When I met my wife, there was an excitement at the possibility of a relationship, but love did not develop until I began to get to know her. The more we shared our lives with each other the more our love for each other deepened.

The Bible will allow your child to become acquainted with God. She will learn that God is the creator of all things, including herself. She will see that God has a family that He protects and cares for. It will be clear that God is displeased when His children disobey. Your child will discover that God is her shepherd, peacemaker, healer, provider, teacher, and comforter.

As she comes to know God, her love for God will deepen because it is evident that God loved her first. 1 John 4:19 says, *"We love, because He first loved us."* As the Bible reveals God's love, your child will respond with love.

The Bible is also a source of wisdom, strength, and guidance. It will speak to specific circumstances in her life to encourage her and give him direction. As your child reads the Bible, she is learning that there are practical truths relevant to her life. These truths will point her in the right direction and help her love God with her whole heart.

1 Children obey your parents in the Lord for this is right.
2 Honor your father and mother (which is the first commandment with a promise),
3 that it may be well with you, and that you may live long on the earth. (Ephesians 6:1-3)

21 But examine everything carefully; hold fast to that which is good;
22 abstain from every form of evil. (1 Thessalonians 5:20, 21)

Do not be deceived: "Bad company corrupts good morals." (1 Corinthians 15:33)

The Bible will help your child to live as God would have her live because it outlines what God expects of her. A remembrance of scriptural principles will guide her away from sin. Psalm 119:11 says, *"Thy Word have I treasured in my heart, that I may not sin against thee."*

Scripture will not only show her what God considers sin so she can avoid it, but it will also equip her to do good.

16 All Scripture is inspired by God and profitable for teaching, for reproof, for correction, for training in righteousness;
17 that the man of God may be adequate, equipped for every good work (2 Timothy 3:16, 17)

Because God inspired the Bible, the Bible is powerful. As your child reads, she is taught where she is wrong (reproof), shown how to change her behavior (correction), pointed in the proper direction (training in righteousness), and equipped to accomplish good works.

Is She Learning to Pray?

Prayer does not come easily to most of us. Even the disciples had some difficulty. *"And it came about that while He (Jesus) was praying in a certain place, after He had finished, one of His disciples said to Him, 'Lord teach us to pray...'" (Luke 11:1)* The disciples were observing Jesus' prayer time, felt inadequate, and appointed one spokesman to ask for instruction.

Praying will not come naturally to your child; she will learn from your teaching, your example, and her practice. Teach her about prayer, show her how to pray, and help her practice.

Because she is a child, only the basics should be presented to her. There is no need to charge off into the subjects of intercession or praying in the spirit. Stick to what prayer is, why it is important, and how to do it.

What is prayer? Prayer is talking and listening to God. It is a conversation where we express our gratitude to God, confess our sins, present our requests, and listen to what God wants to say. When we pray, God is there with us. *"The Lord is near to all who call upon Him, to all who call upon Him in truth." (Psalm 145:18)* God is not there merely to listen; He speaks, making prayer a conversation between friends. "And while they were ministering to the Lord and fasting, the Holy Spirit said, *'Set apart for Me Barnabas and Saul for the work to which I have called them.'" (Acts 13:2)*

Why is prayer important to your child? It is important because it is the foundation of every successful Christian endeavor. Prayer is your child's means to talk to God, Who is the ruler of the universe and King of heaven. It is your child's way to express thanks to God and tap into God's wisdom and provision.

Prayer is important because without it your child could not receive from God. "...You do not have because you do not ask. You ask and do not receive because you ask with wrong motives, so that you may spend it on your treasures." (James 4:2, 3) If we could not ask, we would not receive.

Prayer is important because through it your child can receive everything he needs. "And my God shall supply all your needs according to His riches in glory in Christ Jesus." (Philippians 4:19) Prayer is his means to experience the joy of having his needs met. John 16:24 says, "Until now you have asked for nothing in My name; ask, and you will receive, that your joy may be made full."

Prayer is important because when your child talks to God, God listens and your child can count on God to respond. 1 John 5:14, 15 tells us that we can have confidence in our prayers. "And this is the confidence we have before Him, that, if we ask anything according to His will, He hears us. And if we know that He hears us in whatever we ask, we know that we have the requests which we have asked from Him."

How should your child pray? Prayer is not a one two three process, check list, or formula. It is not limited to one posture. It may be done while sitting, kneeling, driving, or running. His eyes may be open, closed (not while driving), or raised toward heaven. His prayer may be unspoken, softly spoken, or very loud. Prayer time is not just during designated hours of the day.

Prayer flows from a relationship with God and is not a rehearsed procedure. If her relationship with God is open and honest, prayer is a heart to heart conversation, not just a speech.

There are several things your child should know about prayer:

1. She needs to take time to pray regularly.
2. Regardless of her bodily posture, she must be on her knees in her heart.
3. Her attention should be on God.
4. *She must talk to God, the Father, in Jesus' name. "And in that day, you will ask Me (Jesus) no question. Truly, truly, I say to you, if you shall ask the Father for anything, He will give it to you in My name. Until now you have asked for nothing in My name; ask, and you will receive, that your joy may be made full." (John 16:23, 24)*

Praying in Jesus' name means coming to God based on knowing His Son personally. We come not on the merit of our own name but through Jesus' name.

5. She should use prayer to communicate with God not to impress others.

6. She should take time to listen.

7. Her prayer should include expression of his love for God, confession for his sins, thanksgiving, and requests for his and other people's needs.

8. Jesus gives us instruction concerning prayer in Matthew 6:5-15.

5 "And when you pray, you are not to be as the hypocrites; for they love to stand and pray in the synagogues and on the street corners, in order to be seen by men. Truly I say to you, they have their reward in full.

6 "But you, when you pray, go into your inner room, and when you have shut your door, pray to your Father who is in secret, and your Father who sees in secret will repay you.

7 "And when you are praying, do not use meaningless repetition, as the Gentiles do, for they suppose that they will be heard for their many words.

8 "Therefore, do not be like them; for your Father knows what you need, before you ask Him.

9 "Pray, then in this way: 'Our Father who art in heaven, Hallowed be Thy name.

10 'Thy kingdom come. Thy will be done, on earth as it is in heaven.

11 'Give us this day our daily bread.

12 'And forgive us our debts, as we also have forgiven our debtors.

13 'And do not lead us into temptation, but deliver us from evil. (For Thine is the kingdom, and the power, and the glory, forever, Amen.)'

14 "For if you forgive men for their transgressions, your heavenly Father will also forgive you.

15 "But if you do not forgive men, then your Father will not forgive your transgressions."

Teach your child how to pray. Show her how to pray by your example. Help her practice. Good prayer habits, coupled with a salvation experience, will make your child's prayer time a success. Now, is the time to help her develop good prayer habits. Later, when her salvation is secure, she will be equipped for effective prayer.

Is She Learning to Turn to God for Help?

Even a small child encounters situations where she needs God's help. She may feel lonely when dad is away on a business trip. She may be anxious to be picked up from the babysitter. She may be frightened by a loud noise or may hurt when she falls from her bike.

Use these circumstances to direct her to God for help. Teach her that, when dad is gone, God is her friend and will bring dad home safely. Teach her to ask God to comfort him at the babysitter's and to trust God to protect her when frightened. Teach her that God soothes and heals when she is hurt. *"My help comes from the Lord, who made heaven and earth." (Psalm 121:2)*

Is She Learning to Talk About the Lord and Include Him in Her Thoughts and Plans?

Most Christians include God in their thoughts and plans on Sunday. However, when Monday arrives, many Christians do not spend much time thinking about God until the next Sunday. On the other hand, during their normal weekly routine, they frequently think about their friends. Just as they include their friends in their thoughts and plans all week, they should include God.

Teach your child to talk about God and to include God in her daily thoughts and plans. Your child should learn to speak of God as creator when she sees a budding tree. She should think of God as healer when her friend is sick. Your child should view God as protector when she plans to ride her bike. She should learn to express thanks to God as provider at meal time. God should be called upon as helper when she reads the Bible and prays. God is always there, and your child should be conscious of His constant presence. Teach your child to talk about God and to include God in her daily thoughts and plans.

Is She Learning the Meaning of Faith and Trust?

Worry is one of the most common sins and a major cause of illness. If you worry, it is because you have waived from faith and trust in God. Worry and faith cannot coexist.

We operate in faith very well concerning things we have seen to be dependable repeatedly. For example, when we want to sit down in our homes, we do not ease into the chair, cautiously, worrying if it will support us. We have faith that the chair will hold us, so we plop down. When we want to stop our cars, we do not begin to test the brakes well in advance, worrying if they will work this time. We trust our brakes to do what they have always done.

Just as you have faith in your furniture and car, your child should learn to have faith in God. If anyone or anything is dependable, it is God. Your child does not need to worry if God will "work" this time. Make it a point to show her how trustworthy God is.

Point out to her that when fear came, it also went because God was there; when she was sick, her health was restored because God was working; when she prayed for protection during the car ride to grandmother's, she arrived safely. God is worthy of his faith and trust. Your responsibility is to teach her that when she sits in God's lap, God holds her every time just like her favorite chair holds her every time.

Is She Learning the Joy of the Christian Way of Life?

The joys of the Christian life are numerous and should be brought to your child's attention. Be specific when you are showing your child these joys.

Special friends are an example of a joy you can show your child. Single out one of her friends and tell her why that friend is special. Finish the teaching session by telling her that God gives her special friends to share happiness with her. She should learn that God makes life joyful.

If you are walking with the Lord, there will be many times that you can teach your child the joys of Christian living by sharing what is happening in your life. You can share how your friends are special; why giving your tithe to God is fun; how a specific prayer was answered; about a Scripture that gives you strength or helped you be a blessing to someone else. Your life is an excellent way to educate her concerning Christian joys.

Her life is also an opportunity for you to teach her. Children eagerly display their happiness. When she is happy, tell her how God is responsible for and enjoys her happiness.

God wants His children to have a joyful life. Teach your child that principle from (1) your life, (2) her life, and (3) Scripture. John 10:10 says, *"I (Jesus) came that they might have life, and might have it abundantly."* 2 Peter 1:3 says, *"His divine power has granted to us everything pertaining to life and godliness."*

Do not assume that your child is discovering, by herself, the joys that come from being friends with God. When the opportunity arises, point out that the pleasure is hers because of God. By teaching her the link between God and joy, you are helping her to see a relationship with God as something to be desired. In developing that desire, you are proceeding toward securing his salvation.

Summary: Concept 1. Love God with All Her Heart

There are several things you can do to help your child learn to love God with her whole heart, soul, mind, and strength. You can tell her about God's love and about Jesus' birth and death. You can help her to read the Bible and to pray. You can show her how to turn to God for help and how to include God in her thoughts and plans. You can teach her to have faith in God and assist her in recognizing the joys of the Christian way of life.

Concept 2. Follow God's Will

God created your child to carry out His will. Your child is a result of the work of God, and God wants him to follow His will so that His kingdom receives benefit. *"For we are His workmanship, created in Christ Jesus for good works, which God prepared beforehand, that we should walk in them." (Ephesians 2:10)*

Jesus came, not for selfish reasons, but to do God's will. *"For I (Jesus) have come down from heaven, not to do My own will, but the will of Him who sent Me." (John 6:38)* Because Jesus is our example, we should walk in God's will, also. 1 John 2:6 reads, "the one who says he abides in Him ought himself to walk in the same manner as He walked." Jesus did God's will, and we should do what Jesus did.

Teach your child to be obedient to God's will, so he can be what God created him to be and can accomplish the good works God has prepared for him. Putting aside his own desires to submit to the will of a higher authority will not come naturally. Following God's will is not an inborn trait; it must be learned.

King David, a man after God's own heart, knew it was a learning process to do God's will. He tells us so in Psalm 143:10. *"Teach me to do Thy will, for Thou art my God;"* Be the teacher your child needs so that he learns to follow God's will.

Is He Learning to Behave Properly in Church, God's House?

Part of learning to follow God's will involves developing a respect for God and a desire to act properly in His presence. Church is an ideal setting to teach these two principles.

Teach your child that God is an important person, Who is worthy of his respect. When he goes to church, he will be in God's house with other people who want to meet with God. Out of respect for God, he should behave in a manner that is pleasing to God. Out of respect for other people, his behavior should not be distracting.

He does not have to sit without moving, with eyes locked on the pastor, and hands clasped in his lap. A church service is not a military exercise demanding rigidity and precision, but it does call for good behavior. He should not be allowed to talk, lie on the floor, or walk around. He should, however, be permitted to exhibit behavior less disciplined than an adult.

Your goal is to teach him to respect God and be well behaved in His presence. He should want to behave properly in church out of a respect for God and a desire to please God. He should act in a way that would receive God's approval. By learning these principles in church, he is learning to consider how God would want him to act and then respond appropriately in other situations, also. He is learning to seek and submit to God's will for his life.

Is He Learning to Obey His Parents in Preparation for Later Obedience to God?

I think the most important principle your child can learn related to the concept of following God's will is to obey you. Both the salvation experience and the Christian walk are responses of obedience to God. Your child learns to obey God by obeying you.

God's Word is clear that salvation is a result of obedience to the plan God established for mankind. Romans 10:9, 10 says, "That if you confess with your mouth Jesus as Lord, and believe in your heart that God raised Him from the dead, you shall be saved; for with the heart man believes, resulting in righteousness, and with the mouth he confesses, resulting in salvation." Similarly, 1 John 5:11,12 states, "And the witness is this, that God has given us eternal life, and this life is in His Son. He who has the Son has the life; he who does not have the Son of God does not have the life."

The salvation choice is one of obedience or rejection. If your child is obedient to the Scriptures and believes, then he has the Son and eternal life. If he does not obey, he has neither.

The primary way your child will learn obedience to a God he cannot see is by obeying parents he can see. In teaching him to trust and follow your direction, even when he would rather do something different, he is learning to trust and follow God's direction. For his salvation to be secured, he will have to believe and submit to God's direction. Make sure he is submitting to you now in preparation for later obedience to God.

"Children, obey your parents in the Lord, for this is right. Honor your father and mother (which is the first commandment with a promise), that it may be well with you, and that you may live long

on the earth." (Ephesians 6:1-3 Use the Bible to show your child that his obedience to you is a command from God with a promise to him.

Is He Learning There Are Many Forms of Authority to Which He Must Submit?

Your child should know that God is pleased when he submits to other forms of authority, also. These would include his grandparents, his church and school teachers, the safety patrol, and his friends' parents.

When he submits to authority, he is following God's will because submitting to authority is a principle from God's Word. "Let every person be in subjection to the governing authorities. For there is no authority except from God, and those which exist are established by God. Therefore, he who resists authority has opposed the ordinance of God; and they who have opposed will receive condemnation upon themselves." (Romans 13:1, 2)

Paul, in the book of Titus, speaks to the subject of authority, also. "Remind them to be subject to rulers, to authorities, to be obedient, to be ready for every good deed, to malign no one, to be uncontentious, gentle, showing every consideration for all men." (Titus 3:1, 2)

In submitting to various authority figures, your child is shaping his will to follow what is right, not what the flesh desires. As he is following his teacher's directions to be silent and overcoming the desire to talk, he is preparing himself to follow God's direction to avoid sin. He also is overcoming the desires of his flesh.

Help him learn to submit to human authority in preparation for submitting to the authority of God and His Word. To receive salvation, he must voluntarily be subject to divine authority.

Is He Learning God's Nature Includes Love and Justice?

God is a God of love. He loved us while we were unsaved sinners, and because of that love, He bought us by sending Jesus to the cross. His love is so strong that nothing can separate us from it.

"Who shall separate us from the love of Christ? Shall tribulation, or distress, or persecution, or famine, or nakedness, or peril or sword?... For I am convinced that neither death, nor life, nor angels, nor principalities, nor things present, nor things to come, nor powers, nor height, nor depth, nor any other created thing,

shall be able to separate us from the love of God, which is in Christ Jesus our Lord." (Romans 8:35, 38, 39)

Love is so characteristic of God that 1 John 4:8 says, *"God is love."* Christians do a good job promoting God as being full of love and mercy, but there is another side to His nature; God's justice must be taught, also.

God has given us spiritual laws by which we are to live our lives. When we willfully break those laws, we put ourselves in a position to experience the justice of God. Because God is just, we may have to suffer the consequences of our actions. Galatians 6:7 explains how the process works. "Do not be deceived, God is not mocked; for whatever a man sows, this he will also reap. For the one who sows to his own flesh shall from the flesh reap corruption, but the one who sows to the Spirit shall from the Spirit reap eternal life."

Your child must know that, in addition to being loving, God is just. If he sows good deeds, God is just to reward him, but if he sows deeds not pleasing to God, then God is just to discipline him.

If you are loving and just in your response to his actions, he will learn that God is loving and just, also. Studies prove that your child will assume that God's nature is the same as he perceives your nature to be.

Is He Learning That Sin Has Inevitable Consequences?

Sin is not something to be taken lightly. Sin caused Adam to die, and because of sin, Jesus' death was required to redeem mankind. The Bible says that God hates sin, and it is no wonder why He feels that way. Sin separated God from His creation and led to the sacrifice of His Son to bridge that separation. Your child must know how God feels about sin and what sin can do in his own life.

The consequences of sin are drastic and can be eternal, because sin causes spiritual death. *"For the wages of sin is death, but the free gift of God is eternal life in Christ Jesus our Lord." (Romans 6:23)* If sin is not dealt with through salvation, spiritual death is the eternal consequence.

Because of sin, an eternal decision must inevitably be made. Your child will repent of sin and accept Jesus as Lord, resulting in eternal life in heaven, or he will reject God's provision for sin, resulting in eternal death in hell. Teach your child the eternal consequences of sin.

Not only does sin affect where he will spend eternity, but also it impacts his temporal life on earth. Sin, even if hidden to others, will eventually catch up with him. Numbers 32:23 says, *"...behold, you have sinned against the Lord, and be sure your sin will find you out."*

Sin may bring short term gratification, but its inevitable consequences are not pleasant. *"The soul of transgressors shall eat violence. Good understanding giveth favor: but the way of transgressors is hard." (Proverbs 13:2, 15 KJV)* Teach your child that sin makes this life difficult and can prevent him from enjoying heaven in the next life.

Summary: Concept 2. Follow God's Will

Teach your child to seek and follow God's will by behaving in church, by submitting to your and other's authority, by realizing that God's nature includes justice, and by understanding that sin has inevitable consequences.

Concept 3. Keep God's Commandments

God is worthy of your child's obedience and it is his duty to keep God's commandments. *"Fear God, and keep his commandments: for this is the whole duty of man." (Ecclesiastes 12:13 KJV)* Teach your child that one of his responsibilities as God's creation is to follow the rules God has for his life.

Is He Learning That God's Commandments Are to Free Him Not to Restrict Him?

God has given him laws or commandments to guide his actions. These commandments are not meant to bind and restrict him but are to free him from the consequences of sin we have just discussed under Concept 2. These commandments are for his protection not punishment.

In Jesus' prayer from John 17:17, you can see that God's Word, the Bible, is truth and is given for our benefit to sanctify us. *"Sanctify them in the truth; Thy Word is truth."*

If God's Word is truth, then His commandments found in Exodus 20:1-17 are truth. John 8:31, 32 tells us, *"If you abide in My word, then you are truly disciples of Mine; and you shall know the truth and the truth shall make you free."* Since the commandments are truth, they are meant to set us free.

Teach your child to view the commandments positively as guidelines for his good to set him free from the trouble that comes with sin. He should see God's Word as something he can obey, resulting in blessing, rather than a list of rules to punish him. The commandments are for freedom not restriction. Your child should have a healthy view of them.

Is He Learning to Put God First?

The first commandment is to put no other gods before God. Your child's god is whatever takes number one priority with him. God requires that He must come first.

As a I was growing up, there were Sunday mornings when sleep came before God, and I stayed home from church. There were times during athletic competition when I was more concerned with what people thought about my performance than what God thought. At times like those God was not number one.

Your child does not have to carve an idol, place it in his room, and bow to worship it to have gods before God. Anything that rates higher than God is a violation of the first commandment. It could be a new toy or a favorite sport. Desire for popularity could be his god, or a girlfriend could be number one. Toys, sports, popularity, and girls can all be good things and can even be of high priority. However, they must not come before God.

Show him through your actions that God comes first. Thanking God for your food should come before your desire to eat. Your income should be offered to God first and then it should be spent in other areas. Your first response to a blossoming argument should be to act in a manner pleasing to God, not pleasing to self. Put God first in everything you do.

When your child faces circumstances that require priorities to be set, point him to consider God first. If he has the choice to use foul language and be accepted by a certain friend or keep his speech clean and run the risk of being rejected, help him consider what God would want. No matter how enticing, God demands that nothing come before Him.

Is He Learning Respect for God's Name?

"You shall not take the name of the Lord your God in vain, for the Lord will not leave him unpunished who takes His name in vain." (Exodus 20:7)

Teach your child that God is a name to be spoken respectfully when he prays or when he speaks of God to others. The same guidelines apply to the name Jesus. They are high names and names to be blessed. They are names to be exalted and glorified. King David had the right perspective as recorded in the Book of Psalms.

18 Blessed be the Lord God, the God of Israel, who alone works wonders.
19 And blessed be His glorious name forever; And may the whole earth be filled with His glory. (Psalm 72:18, 19)

1 Praise the Lord! Praise, O servants of the Lord. Praise the name of the Lord.
2 Blessed be the name of the Lord from this time forth and forever.
3 From the rising of the sun to its setting the name of the Lord is to be praised. (Psalm 113:1-3)

The apostle Paul received revelation from God concerning the name Jesus. He shares that with us in his letter to the Philippians.

9 Therefore God also highly exalted Him (Jesus), and bestowed on Him the name which is above every name.
10 that at the name of Jesus every knee should bow, of those who are in heaven and on earth and under the earth. (Philippians 2:9, 10)

Using the names God and Jesus while cursing are obviously vain uses of them, but it is possible to speak them vainly in other ways, also. Any idle use of Their names breaches the second commandment.

I think the most frequent way God's name is taken in vain is to use it void of the respect it carries. People use God or Jesus as filler with no real meaning. "My God, it's raining again." "Oh, God what a mess." "Jesus Christ." "Oh, my God."

God's name should not be used as empty and powerless filler. It carries power and deserves respect. It should only be used by your child when he is intentionally talking to or about God. He should be learning respect for God's name.

Is He Learning to Keep the Sabbath Day Holy?

From the very beginning God established a seventh or Sabbath day for rest from labor and for focusing on His works. God worked the first six days of creation by speaking into existence the heavens, earth, animals and man, but the next day was different. God was not tired, but He ceased work and rested on the seventh day.

1 Thus the heavens and the earth were completed, and all their hosts.

2 And by the seventh day God completed His work which He had done; and He rested on the seventh day from all His work which He had done.
3 Then God blessed the seventh day and sanctified it, because in it He rested from all His work which God had created and made. (Genesis 2:1-3)

The Sabbath was special because God blessed and sanctified it. God set it apart from the other days and, therefore, it was holy. The word holy in Hebrew means set apart for God's purposes.

God had a specific purpose in the Sabbath. It was for the benefit of His finest creation, people. God did not need to rest, but He knew people did. God did not have to reflect on His works, but He knew people would benefit from such reflection.

Jesus told the Pharisees why the Sabbath was established. "And He (Jesus) was saying to them (Pharisees), 'The Sabbath was made for man, and not man for the Sabbath.'" (Mark 2:27) The Sabbath was established for man's benefit.

God in His wisdom set aside a day from routine duties for people's physical, mental, and spiritual recharging. The Sabbath is blessed, sanctified, and a gift from God to us. The Sabbath was made for us.

Teach your child that God made a special day for his benefit. Also, for his good, God gave a commandment to observe the Sabbath. God wants your child to keep the Sabbath as a different day, set apart for God's purposes. Your child should rest, recharge, and reflect on God and what God has done.

God made and will honor the day He blessed and sanctified during creation, if your child will remember that it is a special day and keep it holy. Teach him that God did His part by making the Sabbath, and that man's commandment is to use it properly by resting and reflecting.

Is He Learning to Value Human Life?

People are God's most cherished creation. No matter how unlovely some may be, all people are a masterpiece in God's eyes. King David tells us that in Psalm 139:14. *"I will give thanks to Thee, for I am fearfully and wonderfully made; Wonderful are Thy works and my soul knows it very well."*

Teach your child to view others the way God does. God breathed life into Adam and from Adam, God made Eve. God declared His creation to be "very good". God was pleased with the man and woman He made in His own image. He desired to fellowship with them forever. When they fell away, God bought them back with the blood of His Own Son. God views each person as a priceless creation, and your child should learn to see others with that perspective.

God values human life and gave Moses laws designed to preserve it. The sixth commandment shows God's value of human life. *"You shall not murder." (Exodus 21:13)*

Your child probably will never murder, but he will have ample opportunities to treat others in a way that does not recognize that God values those people as prized possessions. In his relations with others, he should act in a manner that reflects the fact that God loves them so much that He sacrificed Jesus for them.

Is He Learning God's Rules Governing Sexuality?

Your child will eventually be faced with sexual decisions. If he is to obey God's commandments, he must be taught what God's Word says about sex. If he does not understand what God requires and makes his decision based on emotion, he will be in danger.

Sexual sin is not viewed lightly by God, in fact, He hates the misuse of the act He established to produce more of His creation. In the Old Testament the penalty could be death. In the New Testament we are told that it brings God's wrath. *"Therefore, consider the members of your earthly body as dead to immorality, impurity, passion, evil desires, and greed, which amounts to idolatry. For it is on account of these things that the wrath of God will come." (Colossians 3:5, 6)*

There are three types of sexual sin your child should know: Fornication, Adultery, and Homosexuality. He should know that fornication is sex before marriage, adultery is sex with someone other than his wife, and homosexuality is sex with someone of the same gender.

Most likely, fornication will be the greatest temptation of the three, but your child should know that the Bible declares all to be sin. 1 Corinthians 6:9, 10 lets us know that God has no place in His kingdom for fornication, adultery, or homosexuality. *"Or do you not know that the unrighteous shall not inherit the kingdom of God? Do not be deceived; neither <u>fornicators</u>, nor idolaters, nor <u>adulterers</u>, nor effeminate, nor <u>homosexuals</u>, nor thieves, nor revilers, nor swindlers, shall inherit the Kingdom of God."*

God wants your child to abstain from sex before marriage so that what is meant for marriage is saved for marriage. There are heavy prices to be paid for the sin of fornication: disease, unwanted pregnancy, severed relationships, decreased fellowship with God, and the impact of receiving God's discipline.

Paul tells us how God feels about fornication in his letter to the Hebrews. *"Let marriage be held in honor among all, and let the marriage bed be undefiled; for fornicators and adulterers God will judge." (Hebrews 13:4)* Your child should know that sex before marriage is wrong and will bring God's judgment.

"You shall not commit adultery." (Exodus 20:14) God designed the family structure to be intimate and faithful. The sexual act was created by God for a couple's benefit within the marriage relationship. Husband and wife are to leave their respective families to start their own. That new family grows as they become one flesh through sex. God approves of the intimate sexual act in marriage.

God demands faithfulness in marriage between husband and bride just as He demands faithfulness between Christ and His bride, the church. Teach your child about the faithfulness God requires.

God's anger burns against homosexuality. He destroyed the city of Sodom because of that sin. The book of Romans communicates God's feelings toward homosexuality. "For this reason, God gave them over to degrading passions; for their women exchanged the natural function for that which is unnatural, and in the same way also the men abandoned the natural function of the woman and burned in their desire towards one another, men with men committing indecent acts and receiving in their own persons the due penalty of their error." (Romans 1:26, 27) These verses clearly reveal that God does not approve of homosexuality.

Be certain that your child learns God's rules concerning homosexuality. He should understand that God and judges that sin.

Sexual sin is not limited to an external act but occurs even with the internal thought. Jesus gives us a commentary on the seventh commandment in the New Testament book of Matthew. "You have heard that it was said, 'You shall not commit adultery'; but I say to you, that everyone who looks on a woman to lust for her has committed adultery with her already in his heart." (Matthew 5:27, 28)

People who indulge in impure desire have already committed sin in their hearts and are in danger of performing that sin with their bodies. Such was the case with King David. He saw Bathsheba, committed adultery in his heart by lusting for her, and fulfilled his desire by bringing his body into sin.

Your child must know that entertaining lustful thoughts is sin and that those thoughts put him in danger of completing the act. Thought becomes desire. Desire becomes action. Action becomes habit. Habit becomes lifestyle. Teach your child to break the chain at the point of temptation before thoughts become desire.

The Bible tells us that temptation is not sin until we desire to carry out the temptation. *"For we do not have a high priest (Jesus) who cannot sympathize with our weaknesses, but one who has been tempted in all things as we are, yet without sin."* *(Hebrews 4:15)* Because Jesus was tempted but remained sinless, we know temptation is not sin.

When Jesus was tempted, He knew that the temptation violated godly principles. Jesus refused to play with the temptation and discarded it, allowing Him to avoid sin. Your child should learn God's principles governing sex so that when temptation comes he recognizes its error and casts it aside preventing sin.

Is He Learning to Be Truthful and Honest?

"You shall not bear false witness against your neighbor." *(Exodus 20:16)* This commandment could be expanded to, "Do not lie under any circumstances." Lying is readily tolerated in our society. For some reason, we think it is acceptable to have someone tell the person on the telephone that we are not home, when we are. We regularly say, "I will try to be there", when we have no intention of going. We are habitual exaggerators, making the good better and the bad worse. All these examples are lies in God's eyes.

A Christian should be true to his word. He should be one hundred percent factual. It would be great if everyone meant what they said with nothing hidden and no deceit.

Jesus said He is the Truth. For your child to be Christ like, he will have to tell the truth. If he says he will take out the trash, he should take it out. He should admit his mistakes instead of covering up with a lie. He should not overstate his accomplishments. Everything he says should be true.

6 Listen, for I shall speak noble things; and the opening of my lips will produce right things.
7 For my mouth will utter truth; and wickedness is an abomination to my lips.
8 All the utterances of my mouth are in righteousness; there is nothing crooked or perverted in them.

9 They are all straight forward to him who understands, and right to those who find knowledge. (Proverbs 8:6-9)

Honesty extends beyond speaking truthful words. It is possible to be silent and be dishonest. Let's imagine that your child sees a copy of tomorrow's test on his teacher's desk and copies several questions during lunch. The teacher discovers that the papers have been disturbed and asks the class if anyone knows who looked at the test. Your child is silent. In silence, he copied the test, being dishonest once. By not answering the teacher's question, he was dishonest a second time. Your child should be honest even when honesty may lead to punishment.

When my son was 15 months old, he displayed some brave honesty. He had a bear shaped night light in his room that he knew should not be pulled from the wall. We were playing in his closet, and he walked out into his room, leaving me alone. I could not see what he was doing, but in a couple of minutes he returned with the night light. He looked up at me and said, "Daddy, spanking." That is honesty.

Your child's goal is to be truthful and honest always. Cheating is dishonest, as is pretending to be sick to stay home from school or church. Honesty has no room for sneaking a cookie or peeking into Christmas presents. In all areas of life, teach your child to be truthful and honest.

Is He Learning the Relative Insignificance of Materialism?

I have heard others remark that more is said about materialism in the Bible than any other subject. Even God's commandments address materialism twice.

You shall not steal. (Exodus 20:15)

You shall not covet...anything that belongs to your neighbor. (Exodus 20:17)

Many people are caught up in a quest for possessions. They desire better and more expensive homes, cars, clothes, and "stuff". I have not coveted those things, but I have desired a larger bank account. That is materialistic, too.

We are a financial oriented society. We spend much of our efforts accumulating things that are temporal. They will not last; they will not survive the transition into eternity. Compared with spiritual accomplishments, material possessions are insignificant because that which is spiritual is eternal, while material things will pass away.

Jesus gave us good advice concerning the things we stockpile in our lives.

19 "Do not lay up for yourselves treasures upon earth, where moth and rust destroy, and where thieves break in and steal.
20 "But lay up for yourselves treasures in heaven, where neither moth nor rust destroys, and thieves do not break in or steal;
21 for where your treasure is, there will your heart be also."
33 "But seek first His kingdom and His righteousness; and all these things shall be added unto you." (Matthew 6:19-21, 33)

Jesus' motive is not to prevent us from having things but to prevent things from having us. In the gospels, Jesus had a conversation with an individual described as a rich, young ruler. Upon questioning, the individual revealed morality of the highest quality. He had kept all the commandments since he was a youth. Then, Jesus made a request of the individual that brought out his problem. Jesus asked the rich, young ruler to sell all that he owned and follow Him. The rich, young ruler was unable to follow because "things had him."

If we seek God first, He will make sure material things are added. Seeking God's kingdom first puts everything in proper balance. God is utmost; things are added; we have things, but they do not have us. The right balance keeps riches from luring us into trouble.

Nothing is wrong with riches if they are kept in the correct perspective. Many people misquote 1 Timothy 6:10, saying, "Money is the root of all evil." The correct quotation is, *"For the love of money is a root of all sorts of evil, and some by longing for it have wondered away from the faith, and pierced themselves with many a pang."* Evil comes when money is loved.

Abraham and Solomon were two of the wealthiest men this world will ever know. Both were made rich by God, and the Bible says that God delights in the prosperity of His servants. From the examples of Abraham and Solomon, we know that there is nothing inherently wrong with riches. Their riches were a blessing and not evil because a healthy perspective existed. God came before riches, and riches were not loved or longed for. Trouble begins when we allow riches to deceive us into loving and longing for material possessions.

1 Timothy, chapter six, gives us a second piece of advice to add to do not love money. *"Instruct those who are rich in this*

present world not to be conceited or to fix their hope on the uncertainty of riches, but on God, who richly supplies us with all things to enjoy." (1` Timothy 6:17)

The Christian attitude is to fix our hope on God because He is certain. We should not trust in riches because they are uncertain and deceiving. When we place our trust in God, He will supply us with things to enjoy. When we trust riches, we are falling for deception.

Riches promise ease, comfort, prestige, and happiness. They claim to be the answer to a fulfilled life, but riches are deceitful and their promises are empty.

In Mark 4:18, 19, Jesus calls riches deceitful. "And others are the ones on whom seed was sown among thorns; these are the ones who have heard the word, and the worries of the world, and the deceitfulness of riches, and the desires for other things enter in and choke the word and it becomes unfruitful."

Riches pretend to offer a harvest of abundant life, but instead, bring a crop of evil and make the existing harvest unfruitful. Riches can be like thorns that choke out good things in our lives. Jesus says riches may choke the Word and prevent it from producing the fruit it is designed to produce. Riches, though insignificant in eternity, are dangerous in this life.

Be certain your child knows that coveting or stealing someone's possessions is sin and displeasing to God. Teach him that he is asking for trouble if he loves and fixes his hope on material things. Most importantly, he must understand that God always comes before things, and materialism is insignificant compared with God.

Is He Learning to Follow the Dictates of His Own Conscience?

God has given your child a mechanism to sort out right from wrong. It resides in his mind, and we refer to it as his conscience. The conscience comes partially programmed and is enhanced by learning to share toys, not touch the stereo, and not kick others.

When a choice is present, the conscience will prod your child to assist him in making a yes or no decision. The flesh also supplies advice, and a battle results ending with your child selecting which to follow conscience or flesh.

Look at an example. Your child has been told that God is pleased when he shares and that one way he can share is to let others use his toys. He has a friend over to play with his trucks. Your child is pushing his cement mixer and stops to switch to his dump truck. The dump truck is across the room where his friend is playing with the pickup. Several feet before your child arrives at the dump truck, his friend releases the pickup and begins pushing the dump truck. A choice must be made. Will he let his friend continue to play with the toy he wants, or will he insist on using the dump truck?

The conscience and flesh begin offering advice. The conscience reminds him that sharing pleases God and points out that his friend had that truck first. The flesh is opposed. It shouts, "That truck is yours and you want it, so take it!"

Your responsibility is to help your child refuse the advice of the flesh and follow the dictates of his conscience. At first, each time you see him succeed reward him with praise and a hug. Later in the learning process, wait until his friend leaves and tell him you noticed how he shared and that it pleased you and God.

When he fails, have a short teaching session with him. Your objective is to develop in him a desire to please God that causes him to do what is right even if it differs from what he wants.

Show him in the Bible how other people have the same battle between doing what is right and what is wrong. Romans 7:14-25 is an excellent example.

14 For we know that the Law is spiritual; but I am of flesh, sold into bondage to sin.

15 For that which I am doing, I do not understand; for I am not practicing what I would like to do, but I am doing the very thing I hate.

16 But if I do the very thing I do not wish to do, I agree with the Law, confessing that it is good.

17 So now, no longer am I the one doing it, but sin which indwells me.

18 For I know that nothing good dwells in me, that is, in my flesh; for the wishing is present in me, but the doing of the good is not.

19 For the good that I wish, I do not do; but I practice the very evil that I do not wish.

20 But if I am doing the very thing I do not wish, I am no longer the one doing it, but sin which dwells in me.

21 I find then the principle that evil is present in me, the one who wishes to do good.

22 For I joyfully concur with the law of God in the inner man,

23 but I see a different law in the members of my body, waging war against the law of my mind, and making me a prisoner of the law of sin which is in my members.

24 Wretched man that I am! Who will set me free from the body of this death?
25 Thanks be to God through Jesus Christ our Lord! So then, on the one hand I myself with my mind am serving the law of God, but on the other, with my flesh the law of sin.

He should know that even though the battle is fierce he can win if he asks God to be his helper. With God's assistance, he can successfully choose to follow the dictates of his conscience.

Concept 4. Love Others as Herself

A child is born with an automatic concern for her needs. She is totally dependent on others to fulfill her desires, and she learns that crying gains the response she seeks. She cries when she is hungry, not because she wants others to receive a blessing from ministering to her, but because she wants her needs met. She is concerned with only one person, herself.

As she grows older, she should be taught that other people deserve her concern, also. She may enjoy pounding grandmother with a spoon, but she needs to see that there is another person involved who may feel differently about the game that pleases her. Her perspective should enlarge to include others in her thought processes.

There are two familiar Scriptures that are the basis for considering other people and their feelings. Jesus spoke both statements.

"And just as you want men to treat you, treat them in the same way." (Luke 6:31) Relationships would rarely be hurt, if we always contemplated how we would want others to act toward us before we acted toward them. This advice from Jesus is so important that we call it the Golden Rule.

The second Scripture is found in Mark 12:31. Our fourth concept Love Others as Herself is extracted from this verse.

29 Jesus answered, "The foremost (commandment) is, 'Hear, O Israel; The Lord our God is one Lord;
30 and you shall love the Lord your God with all your heart, and with all your soul, and with all your mind, and with all your strength.'
31 "The second is this, 'You shall love your neighbor as yourself.' There is no commandment greater than these." (Mark 12:29-31)

Is She Learning to Love Herself?

Your child must first love herself, if she is to properly love others, as herself. If she doesn't love herself, she has no basis to adequately love others. Self-love is a product of self-image, and she will develop her self-image by observing how you and other people feel about her.

If you communicate that she is infallible, her self-image will be inflated. If she perceives that you see her as inferior, she will share that perception. But, if she knows you see and appreciate her good qualities and accept her despite her not so good qualities, then she will accept herself and have a healthy self-image.

There are several things to consider in your plan to help your child develop a healthy self-esteem. Seven suggestions follow.

(1) Your first step in helping her love herself is to get your own heart right toward her. You must love her deeply, even though she is less than perfect. Love her regardless of her faults, inadequacies, and imperfections.

Picture God loving you. Does He love you even though you have flaws? Does He love you even though you are ordinary, rather than a super child? Does He love you even when you don't act like His child should? Let God's love be your model. Love your child the way God loves you, warts and all.

My Christian self-image is healthy and in balance because of how my Father, God, sees me. I see myself as sinful and unspectacular in His Kingdom, but He loved me before I knew Him, calls me son despite my sin, and views my role in His Kingdom as spectacular. I derive my Christian self-concept from my Father. I have great worth to Him just the way I am.

Your child is observing how you feel about her, and her self-image is being built, piece by piece, from what she sees. Let her see love, understanding, acceptance, and respect. Let her know that you see him as having self-worth just the way she is.

Take seriously your responsibility to help her love herself. Do not let less significant things prevent you from offering your child the time it takes to build a healthy self-image. You can either equip her with the ability to love others as herself or leave her unable to do so. The determining factor will be the quality of your interaction with her.

(2) There are three common self-esteem assassins that you should be aware of so that you can prevent them from having the opportunity to stalk your child. They can cause your child to question her worth and destroy her ability to love herself. You can choose to deny entrance into your family to each of the three.

The first self-concept killer is one that seems to get worse each day in America; fatigue and time pressure. Schedules are full to over flowing. Energy supplies are depleted by our jobs, church duties, chores at home, and community activities. When it comes to building a child's self-image and securing her salvation, there is often no time or energy left.

The result of no time and no energy is no effort, and our children are paying the price. Remove from your schedule the overtime, bowling league, community organization, and church duty excess. All can be important, but the success of your child's entire life, including her salvation, may depend on your interaction with her.

A second potential destroyer of your child's self-image is speaking insensitive comments in front of her. Nothing can be more harmful to your child's ability to love herself than to hear you describe all her inadequacies to someone else. "Suzie's a cute kid except for her ears." "Her brother was easy to raise but she's killing us." "I wish she was as smart as the other boys and girls in her class." "She's always so moody; I wish she was a boy."

Do not assume that she is not affected just because she is little. She may not even give indication that she heard, but you can count on her self-image reflecting your remarks. Each insensitive comment attaches a piece of unhealthiness to her view of herself.

The third assassin you should be aware of is competition for your love. A child often feels like she must compete for your love when a new born brother or sister comes into the world. The amount of attention she receives diminishes immediately, and she is not old enough to understand why. In her eyes, she no longer is loved because the "new one" is better. If the situation is left unexplained, her self-concept may be damaged.

Take time to show love to the older child. Explain that babies need a lot of attention because they are helpless, and tell her that you did the same things for her when she was a baby. Help her to express her feelings so that you can understand her misconceptions.

I think the most successful way to protect her self-esteem from scars of competition is to take time to express your love for her in ways that provide her status for being older. Take her to places she enjoys, explaining that the baby is too young to go. Show pride in her abilities, reminding her that the baby cannot do those things. Help her enjoy her seniority and independence.

Protect her self-concept from those things that can inflict lasting damage:

(A) Revamp your schedule so that fatigue and time pressure do not prevent you from spending quality time with your child.

(B) Do not subject her to insensitive comments.

(C) Keep her from being a loser in competition for your love.

(3) Now that we have talked about protecting your child's self-image, let us look at the flip side, over protection. Consistent with almost everything in life, self-esteem building requires a balance.

Zero protection allows unnecessary hurt and too much protection interferes with development. When your child was learning to walk, you did not always follow her around with your hands under her arms so that she never fell. If you had done so, her development would have been hindered. When her toddler peers were walking, she would have still been clutching on to you.

A balance was necessary; you protected her from walking down stairs, but you let her struggle and fall on safe surfaces. Because of that balance, she developed on schedule without serious damage.

Other areas of development should be approached similarly. Protect her from obvious assassins to his self-esteem, but do not let overprotection hinder her growth. If her peers are growing up and she is still clutching onto you, you have set her up for target practice on her self-concept.

Comments like, "Mommy's girl" and "Baby", will greatly restrict her ability to accept and love herself. If your child is behind in social and emotional development, her classmates will notice. She will not enjoy being the center of attention. Protect her from your desire to overprotect her.

(4) Another way you can protect and develop her image of herself is to emphasize her strengths to counterbalance her weaknesses. All of us have weaknesses. If we meditated on them, we would have self-concept problems. Those potential problems are overcome by realizing that even though we are not skilled in some areas, we do other things well.

Your responsibility is to help your child find the skills that will compensate for her weaknesses. Throughout junior high school, my social skills were behind my classmates, but my athletic skills compensated for my weakness. I knew I was not proficient socially, but I saw myself as having worth because I did something else well.

Your child may have musical talent or artistic ability. She may have leadership skills for school clubs or the church youth group. Mechanical aptitudes may be her strong point, or her personality may be charismatic. Whatever her counterbalancing strengths are, they need to be discovered and developed. Help her to find and use them.

(5) A fifth way to protect her self-image is to steer her away from being too critical of herself. Faults should not be ignored, but a steady stream of self-criticism only hampers her ability to love herself.

Constant focus on her deficiencies will cause her to see herself as one big weakness. Excessive inward criticism becomes a habit that dismantles her self-image every time it is turned loose. If she vocalizes her self-criticism to others, they, too, will see her as inferior.

Teach your child to accept blame for her mistakes and to realize that she is not exceptional at all of life's possibilities, but guide her away from constantly battering her self-esteem. Constant self-criticism accomplishes nothing constructive but can prohibit her from loving others if she learns to dislike herself.

(6) Your child certainly will act in ways that require discipline. The way you choose to handle misbehavior will impact her self-image. Your goal is to correct your child's behavior without damaging her self-worth.

Discipline should begin with establishing behavior guidelines. In our society, we call them rules and laws. Your child must know what is expected of her before you can correct her fairly.

Speed limit signs are posted to let drivers know what is expected of them. When a driver exceeds the allowed speed, a police officer can justly issue monetary discipline. If there were no guidelines, fairness would not exist.

Establish general guidelines and detail them as situations present themselves. A general guideline would be to behave nicely at the dinner table. If your child throws peas at the dog, add detail to the general rule before you discipline her.

Once predetermined rules are understood, discipline can be executed justly. Punishment is initiated by you when the pre-established rules are intentionally broken.

If your child chooses to pick a fight with you by throwing peas at the dog, do not disappoint her by backing down. Immediately win the battle. Briefly tell her what she did wrong and that you are going to punish her, because that is what God expects of you. Follow up with love and explain that you discipline her to help her obey God's commands for her life.

There are Scriptures that you can share with her to help her understand what God expects of her and what God expects of you.

"Children, obey your parents in the Lord, for this is right. Honor your father and mother (which is the first commandment with a promise), that it may be well with you, and that you may live long on the earth." (Ephesians 6:1-3)

"He who spares his rod hates his son, but he who loves him disciplines him diligently." (Proverbs 13:24)

The Bible has much say about discipline. Of course, the advice you find there should be your primary guidance. Some of the advice found in God's Word follows.

GOD IS OUR EXAMPLE

5 and you have forgotten the exhortation which is addressed to you as sons, "My son, do not regard lightly the discipline of the Lord, nor faint when you are reproved by Him;

6 For those whom the Lord loves he disciplines, and He scourges every son whom he receives."

7 It is for discipline that you endure; God deals with you as with sons; for what son is there whom his father does not discipline?

8 But if you are without discipline, of which all have become partakers, then you are illegitimate children and not sons.

9 Furthermore, we had earthly fathers to discipline us, and we respected them; shall we not much rather be subject to the Father of spirits, and live? (Hebrews 12:5-9)

ADVICE TO CHILDREN

Children, be obedient to your parents in all things, for this is well pleasing to the Lord. (Colossians 3:20)

ADVICE TO PARENTS

Foolishness is bound up in the heart of a child; The rod of discipline will remove it far from him. (Proverbs 22:15)

15 The rod and reproof give wisdom, but a child who gets his own way brings shame to his mother.

16 When the wicked increase, transgression increases; But the righteous will see their fall.

17 Correct your son, and he will give you comfort; He will also delight your soul. (Proverbs 29:15-17)

13 Do not hold back discipline from the child, Although you beat him with the rod, he will not die.

14 You shall beat him with the rod, and deliver his soul from Sheol. (Proverbs 23:13, 14)

PROPER DISCIPLINE

4 He must be one who manages his own household well, keeping his children under control with all dignity
5 (but if a man does not know how to manage his own household, how will he take care of the church of God?); (1 Timothy 3:4, 5)

And, fathers, do not provoke your children to anger; but bring them up in the discipline and instruction of the Lord. (Ephesians 6:4)

Fathers, do not exasperate your children, that they may not lose heart. (Colossians 3:21)

Swift, calm discipline for willful disobedience of pre-established guidelines will not mar your child's self-concept, especially when followed by a big dose of love and assurance. Discipline is not harmful unless it includes rejection, disrespect, ridicule, excessive punishment, verbal abuse, or threats to withdraw love.

To summarize, to correct behavior without damaging self-worth:

(A) Establish guidelines.

(B) Win the battle she chooses to initiate.

(C) Follow up with love.

(7) A seventh way to help your child develop a healthy self-esteem is to help her compete in a world that emphasizes beauty and brains. Nothing can be more detrimental to your child's self-concept than to be called ugly or stupid by her peers.

When my permanent teeth came in, they were not straight. One eye tooth was farther recessed than the others. My parents sacrificed to pay for braces that would improve my appearance.

As I look back, I can see what a wise decision they made. Some of my classmates were not helped to compete in an environment that scrutinizes physical appearance. They were called "fang" and "snaggle tooth", which resulted in painful blows to their self-images.

Physical appearance should not be overemphasized, but in a world so critical of beauty, you can make reasonable efforts to help your child compete. Orthodontics and dermatology can do wonders for her self-image.

Children who are slow learners are also targets for ridicule. Help your child compete by finding tutorial assistance or by clearing your schedule to teach her yourself. The scars you may prevent will be worth the sacrifice.

It is unfortunate that our society values beauty and brains so highly, but such are the facts. A little help from you can allow your child to receive good scores in front of life's many judges. Help her compete.

Self-image is very fragile, and your child's ability to love others is dependent on her ability to love herself. In helping her build a healthy view of herself, consider the seven areas we have discussed.

(1) Let her know you have a good image of her.

(2) Do not let fatigue, time pressure, insensitive comments, or competition for your love destroy her self-esteem.

(3) Do not let overprotection prevent normal development.

(4) Develop her strengths to counterbalance her weaknesses.

(5) Guide her away from excessive self-criticism.

(6) Discipline to shape her behavior without damaging her self-worth.

(7) Help her compete in the contest of beauty and brains.

In this chapter, we have covered a lot of material since stating our purpose. Now would be a good time to restate that purpose. We are looking at post-birth activities that provide spiritual training for our children to direct them toward God and godly values. The object is to train them in the way God wants them to go, so when they are older, they will choose to live by what they have been taught. The ultimate purpose is to move them in the direction of the cross and to secure their salvation.

Is She Learning Not to Be Selfish and Demanding?

We have looked at one side of helping your child love others as herself; she must learn to love herself. The other side involves taking her eyes off herself, to see the needs, and sense the feelings of others. One way you can assist her is to direct her away from being selfish and demanding.

The nature of children is to be self-centered. I have heard that there are some who are not, but I have never seen one. Perhaps you can send a picture of one to me, if you discover such a child.

Because God wants your child to be God centered instead of selfish, and obedient rather than demanding, you need to redirect her focus. Teach her to share and to refrain from insisting on her own way. These are values that will help her submit to God in salvation and service.

The second chapter of Philippians gives us direction concerning selfishness. "Do nothing from selfishness or empty conceit, but with humility of mind let each of you regard one another as more important than himself; do not merely look out for your own personal interests, but also for the interest of others." (Philippians 2:3, 4)

The Bible also warns of the damages of selfishness. *"For where jealousy and selfish ambition exist, there is disorder and every evil thing." (James 3:16)* It is easy to see that it is important that you teach your child not to be selfish and demanding.

Is She Learning to Empathize with the Feelings of Others?

A child is very aware of her feelings. A newborn will cry when she feels hungry. A toddler will become fussy when she feels tired. A preschooler may be upset when left with a babysitter because she feels deserted.

Your child should learn to recognize other's feelings, also, and identify with them. When our son was very young, my wife and I kept the church nursery regularly. It was not uncommon for one child to attempt to comfort another who was crying. Even toddlers have the capacity to empathize with the feelings of others.

The book of Romans instructs us to be aware of and relate to other peoples' feelings. *"Rejoice with those who rejoice, and weep with those who weep." (Romans 12:15)* Several times the Bible states that Jesus had compassion for the multitude because of their needs. Jesus felt what they felt; He empathized with the feelings of others.

Guide your child toward seeing and responding to the feelings of others. Point out what someone else is feeling and suggest a response. "Linda is crying because someone took her doll. Let's share one of your toys with her." Or, "Billy is happy because he learned how to ride his bike. Let's tell him how well he is doing."

Children do not cover up their feelings, as adults do, which makes it easy to find opportunities to recognize their emotional condition. Teach your child to sense and respond to those opportunities.

Is She Learning Not to Gossip and Criticize Others?

All of us want to be spoken of favorably. Have you ever seen someone stop everything she was doing because she heard another person mention her name in conversation? We want others to say nice things about us.

If your child is to love others as herself, she will have to talk about them the way she wants others to talk about her. Gossip and criticism will have to be avoided to accomplish that objective.

I believe that gossip and criticism are primarily learned traits. My toddler son did not by nature gossip and criticize others even though he did talk about others. He repeated what my wife and I said about others. He learned to talk about others by listening to what we said.

He said, "Granddaddy has a lawn mower", not, "Granddaddy is old and gray and wrinkled." He repeated, "Amy has pretty hair", not, "Amy drools and messes her diaper." He didn't gossip and criticize because he had not learned to do so.

Because gossip and criticism are not proper in God's eyes, you must set an example that does not teach your child to practice them. Romans 1:28-32 clearly shows us how God sees gossips and criticizers.

28 And just as they did not see fit to acknowledge God any longer, God gave them over to a depraved mind, to do those things which are not proper.
29 being filled with all unrighteousness, wickedness, greed, malice; full of envy, murder, strife, malice; they are gossips,
30 slanderers, haters of God, insolent, arrogant, boastful, inventors of evil, disobedient to parents,
31 without understanding, untrustworthy, unloving, unmerciful;
32 and, although they know the ordinances of God, that those who practice such things are worthy of death, they not only do the same, but also give hearty approval to those who practice them.

Teach your child to speak favorably about others in the same manner that she wants others to talk about her. It is part of learning to love others as herself.

To help your child learn the spiritual concept of loving others as herself, teach her to love herself, teach her not to be selfish and demanding, teach her to empathize with the feelings of others, and teach her not to gossip and criticize.

Concept 5. Practice the Fruit of the Spirit

"But the fruit of the Spirit is love, joy, peace, patience, kindness, goodness, faithfulness, gentleness, self-control; against such things there is no law." (Galatians 5:22, 23)

Your child's pre-salvation years should be used to train his mind with godly principles that will set him on the path to eternal life. Learning to practice the fruit of the Spirit will provide training that will point him toward a Christian lifestyle.

Is He Learning to Walk in Love?

We have already discussed the three expressions of love your child should learn. First and foremost, he should love God with his whole heart. Having learned to love God, he will be ready to embrace Jesus as Savior.

Secondly, he should love himself. He should see himself as having worth and know that he is of value to God.

The third way he should learn to walk in love can be taught once he learns to love himself. The third expression of love is to love others as himself.

Is He Learning to Live in the Joy that Never Changes?

Circumstances change. Sometimes everything is going our way and life is grand. Everyone in the family is healthy; the loan on the car was just paid off; we are growing spiritually; church is fulfilling; the IRS tax refund just arrived in the mail.

Other times our world falls apart. A family member is in the hospital; the rent went up one hundred dollars a month; we are spiritually stagnant; church is a test of endurance to get everyone ready and arrive on time; we owe the IRS seven hundred dollars.

We spend most of our lives in the in between area, where circumstances are constantly changing, and most of the time something is wrong.

In a life filled with change and unfavorable events, it is a comfort to know that the most important aspects of life never change. God always loves us; He is ever taking care of us; heaven still awaits us.

If we base our happiness on nonchanging truths, we can live in joy that never changes. Happiness is a roller coaster when founded on temporal circumstances, but it is consistent when backed by the faithfulness of God toward us.

Your child should learn to live in joy that never changes. When he encounters unfavorable circumstances, channel him toward those things that are stable in his life so he learns to rely on the constant, rather than dwelling on the circumstances.

Point out that your love for him is always there. Remind him that you are making sure that all his needs are met. Help him see that he still has friends to play with. You are preparing him to center in on God's love, God's provision, and Christian fellowship so that he can live above circumstances in the joy that never changes.

Is He Learning to Turn to God for Peace in the Midst of Turmoil?

A few weeks ago, a thunder storm passed over my house. The rain beat on the ground, and the wind took my garbage can for a ride down the street. I scurried out into the storm with an umbrella to retrieve the can from the neighbor's yard. The wind turned the umbrella inside out and the rain soaked me. I rescued the kidnapped can and fought my way back to the garage.

Inside the garage, I could still see and hear the storm, but there was peace directly around me. I was sheltered from the turmoil. The garage provided peace in the midst of turmoil.

Your child should learn that God provides peace in the midst of turmoil if we seek Him. The storm may not go away, but God makes a place of calm available, so the storm stays outside and does not rage inside your child.

Take time to pray with your child and ask God to provide peace. Be sure to give God the credit when your child is settled. Tell him that you will help him seek God for peace anytime he is in the midst of turmoil. Your purpose is to teach him to set his sights on God instead of the raging sea.

Jesus' disciples encountered a storm and were in danger because all they could see was the raging sea, even though the answer (Jesus) was right there in the boat.

35 And on that day, when evening had come, He said to them, "Let us go over to the other side."

36 And leaving the multitude, they took Him along with them, just as He was, in the boat; and other boats were with Him.

37 And there arose a fierce gale of wind, and the waves were breaking over the boat so much that the boat was already filling up.

38 And He Himself was in the stern, asleep on the cushion; and they awoke Him and said to Him, "Teacher, do You not care that we are perishing?"

39 And being aroused, He rebuked the wind and said to the sea, "Hush, be still." And the wind died down and it became perfectly calm. (Mark 4:35-39)

Jesus did not allow the storm to affect Him, because He knew God was in control. He also called on God's power to stop the raging sea. In the Father's arms there is peace despite what is occurring elsewhere.

There was a man sitting beside a little girl on a train. The train was traveling on tracks anchored into the side of a steep mountain. The rain was pounding on the windows obscuring vision, and the wind was rocking the train back and forth.

The man was amazed at the peacefulness of the little girl. He asked her if she knew how hard it was raining. Her answer was, "Yes". He questioned if she could feel the train rocking and if she knew they were on the side of a mountain. The reply to both was, "Yes".

He asked a final question. "Aren't you afraid?" "No", she responded, "my father is driving the train and he has everything under control."

That is what you need to teach your child. In the midst of turmoil, he can turn to God for peace because God is driving the train of life and has everything under control.

Is He Learning to Be Patient?

Patience is a learned virtue. It is developed by going through unpleasant circumstances. Suppose your child wants a drink of water, but you are shaping hamburger patties. Waiting for you to finish and cleanup is unpleasant to him, but patience can result.

For adults, life is full of situations requiring patience. There are lines at the store, red traffic lights, speed limits, more hours to work until the end of the day, desired purchases that require months of savings, and people wanting to sell you something over the phone.

A child has opportunities to learn patience, also, and it is important that he do so, while the results of impatience are not very severe. He must learn to wait one minute for lunch now, because later the penalty for not waiting one minute for a red light may be death.

Learning patience in daily circumstances teaches patience in waiting on God. I have been guilty of being an impatient spiritual child, stomping my feet because the answer had not yet arrived. I had to learn to wait on the Lord. *"Yet those who wait for the Lord will gain new strength; They will mount up with wings like eagles, They will run and not get tired, They will walk and not become weary." (Isaiah 40:31)*

Sometimes, we miss God's promises because we are impatient. Learning patience may be trying, but it is to our advantage, because it is an essential ingredient in receiving from God. *"For ye have need of patience, that, after ye have done the will of God, ye might receive the promise." (Hebrews 10:36 KJV)*

The benefits of patience to your child are far reaching, because most accomplishments take more than a few minutes to produce. To color a picture between the lines may take thirty minutes. Learning to play the piano well may require years of practice. Most importantly, to develop character that is pleasing to God takes a life time, and patience will help your child achieve that result. *"But let patience have her perfect work, that ye may be perfect and entire, wanting nothing." (James 1:4 KJV)*

Help your child learn to be patient. Purposefully make him wait when he is being demanding. Coach him to the completion of a difficult task when he wants to give up. Patience will, one day, assist him in waiting on God to mold him into someone "perfect and entire, wanting nothing."

Is He Learning to Treat Others with Tenderness?

Kindness, goodness, and gentleness are three closely connected fruits of the Spirit. They all relate to treating others with tenderness. Jesus is the ultimate example of kindness, goodness, and gentleness. He was kind to those who sought Him, performed good works for those in need, and was gentle to even those caught in sins warranting death. Read the gospels to your child, pointing out the tenderness of Jesus toward others.

Children can be very cutting in the nicknames they assign to one another. The girl who is big for her age is labeled, "moose". The boy with big ears becomes known as, "Dumbo". When I was in elementary school, I wore my hair short in a flat top like my dad even though the style at the time was a little longer. One of my kind classmates called me, "square head". Insensitive names are not consistent with kindness, goodness, and gentleness.

Your child's attitude toward others should be shaped to see them as deserving respect. He should be trained to deal with others as Jesus did; always acting in their best interest, despite their spiritual, economic, social, or physical condition.

Ephesians 4:32 KJV reads, "And be ye kind one to another, tenderhearted, forgiving one another, even as God for Christ's sake hath forgiven you." Your child should be learning to act kindly toward all people he encounters.

Is He Learning to Be Faithful?

Faithfulness is an attribute that many adult Christians have not mastered. They come to church when they feel like it and stay home otherwise. They give a little bit of money to God until they want it for themselves. They follow God's laws until it is convenient or pleasurable to break them. They commit themselves to God's service for a short while but abandon the responsibility because it requires consistent effort.

I suspect that they are unfaithful to God because they are unfaithful in the other areas of their lives as well. They stay home from work "sick" because they want a day off. They promise something and do not follow through. They are unreliable and do not stick with what they know is right.

Your child must learn to be faithful in worldly affairs in preparation for faithfulness in spiritual affairs. He should learn to be reliable, to hold fast to what is right, and to make good his promises. What he learns before salvation will help him work out his salvation once he accepts Jesus as Lord.

God expects His children to be faithful and He blesses those who are. "Moreover, it is required in stewards, that a man be found faithful." (1 Corinthians 4:2) "A faithful man will abound with blessings." (Proverbs 28:20) "...Be faithful until death, and I will give you the crown of life." (Revelation 2:10)

Teach your child character that God requires and rewards. Teach him to be faithful.

Is He Learning Self-control?

Self-control is an invaluable attribute to your child. If he controls his impulses to break rules, he will stay out of trouble, and if he pushes himself to do what is right, he will succeed.

Self-control restrains talking when quiet is required. It subdues anger and avoids trouble. Self-control delays curiosity until it is permissible to explore. It prohibits overeating. It puts the flesh under submission when the flesh screams for what is wrong. It stifles improper urges and stops desire in its tracks before it becomes action. Self-control prevents sins.

Paul was acutely aware of the struggle that occurs between self-control and fleshly desire.

15 For that which I am doing, I do not understand; for I am not practicing what I would like to do, but I am doing the very thing I hate.
19 For the good that I wish, I do not do; but I practice the very evil I do not wish.

23 but I see a different law in the members of my body, waging war against the law of my mind, and making me a prisoner of the law of sin which is in my members. (Romans 7:15, 19, 23)

A war raged inside Paul just as it rages inside us and our children. We want to do what is right, but we become enticed by the flesh. Paul knew that the battle for self-control was unrelenting and required constant discipline; the kind of discipline an athlete exercises to excel in his sport.

24 Do you not know that those who run in race all run, but only one receives the prize? Run in such a way that you may win.
25 And everyone who competes in the games exercises self-control in all things. They then do it to receive a perishable wreath, but we an imperishable.
26 Therefore I run in such a way, as not without aim; I box in such a way, as not beating the air.
27 but I buffet my body and make it my slave, lest possibly after I have preached to others, I myself should be disqualified. (1 Corinthians 9:24-27)

Paul knew that self-control was achieved, only, by making his body his slave. Fleshly desires must be buffeted and forced into submission through constant discipline. Sometimes it appears we will never win the conflict, but Paul tells us that we have a helper in the fight for self-control. We have a champion and His name is Jesus.

24 Wretched man that I am! Who will set me free from the body of this death?
25 Thanks be to God through Jesus Christ our Lord! (Romans 7:24, 25)

Self-control is important to your child, not only to keep from doing what is wrong, but also to accomplish what is right. One area where your child can learn self-control toward what is right is in working and carrying responsibility.

A child should not be overburdened with assigned duties, but he should have a few chores that call for the exercise of responsibility. The amount of responsibility should increase over his life time, preparing him for adulthood and service in God's kingdom.

In the twenty-fifth chapter of Matthew, Jesus teaches a parable about responsibility. A man was getting ready to go on a journey, and as part of his preparation, he assigned duties to his three servants. Two of the three servants exhibited self-control and fulfilled their tasks. The third did nothing useful with his responsibility. When the master came home, he was very pleased with those who were faithful, and he expressed wrath toward the one who did nothing. The lesson is clear: teach your child self-control toward responsibility, now, because God expects faithful citizens in His Kingdom. You are preparing your child to function as a loyal servant once his salvation is secured.

Concept 6. Practice Proper Stewardship

When the subject of stewardship is mentioned, people immediately hold on to their wallets, because they think someone is about to ask them for money. Stewardship should be associated with money but should not be limited to that one area.

Stewardship is the process of using everything God has entrusted us with in a manner that is pleasing to Him. We possess resources from His kingdom and must use them wisely. Those resources must be devoted to God first, before our use of them. *"Honor the Lord from your wealth, and from the first of all your produce; so your barns will be filled with plenty, and your vats will overflow with new wine." (Proverbs 3:9,10)*

Since money is thought of first when considering stewardship, we will discuss it first. In Biblical times, farming was the primary way of supporting a family, and monetary stewardship was spoken of in relation to the giving of crops and animals to God.

Today, our giving is through money, but whether we are talking about farm products or money, the scriptural principles governing giving still apply.

"You shall surely tithe all the produce from what you sow, which comes out of the field every year." (Deuteronomy 14:22)

To me, the words, "shall surely", sound like a command that has no exceptions. God demands that we give back to Him a tithe of what He first gives us. Tithe means one tenth.

The Bible says that the first portion of our income is holy to God. The word holy means set apart for God's use. The central truth is that the first tenth of our income is to be set apart and given to ministries in God's kingdom.

"Thus all the tithe of the land, of the seed of the land or of the fruit of the tree, it is the Lord's; it is holy to the Lord." (Leviticus 27:30)

When you bring home a paycheck, sit down with your child and set apart God's tithe. Usually this is done by writing a check to your local church. Explain that God has requirements and blessings that go hand in hand with monetary stewardship. Some excellent verses to share with your child are found in Malachi 3:8-11. God is speaking.

8 "Will a man rob God? Yet you are robbing Me! But you say, 'How have we robbed Thee?' In tithes and contributions."

9 "You are cursed with a curse, for you are robbing Me, the whole nation for you!"

10 "Bring the whole tithe into the storehouse, so that there may be food in My house, and test Me now in this", says the Lord of hosts, "if I will not open for you the windows of heaven, and pour out for you a blessing until there is no more need.

11 "Then I will rebuke the devourer for you, so that it may not destroy the fruits of the ground; nor will your vine in the field cast its grapes", says the Lord of hosts."

God requires the whole tithe and promises blessing that will satisfy all the needs of those who obey. Teach your child the principle of tithing from your example.

Monetary stewardship encompasses more than tithing. Other elements are wise spending, responsible tax paying, saving to spend, and saving for the future.

You can teach your child these through the following example. Execution of the example calls for five jars that will hold money and some form of income for your child, such as an allowance or earnings from chores.

We will assume that your child has earned one dollar for watering the household plants. Exchange the dollar for ten dimes, so he sees that money has practical use and so the mathematics of the example works out evenly.

The first jar is labeled "TITHE" and is used to teach your child that God comes first. Before he designates money for any other reason, the tithe is set apart, holy to God. The first dime goes in this jar.

The next jar is for "TAXES". When your child grows up, he will be required by law to pay taxes on his earnings. Paying taxes is, also, a requirement of God's law as stated in Romans 13:7. *"Render to all what is due them: tax to whom tax is due."* Two dimes go into this jar. Empty this jar regularly as if taxes are being paid. Since you do not have to send this money to the Internal

Revenue Service, you may want to accumulate it and use it to reward your child for faithful monetary stewardship.

The third jar holds money that is "SAVED TO SPEND". Put one dime into this jar. Many of life's purchases require disciplined saving to avoid paying interest on a loan or charge card. I have never known a child who did not want something he did not have such as a new toy or bicycle. This jar is used to save for that type of purchase and for presents for other people. You may choose to have a jar for each saving project and keep a record of progress toward each individual goal. A thermometer that is colored in for each deposit is a useful means of tracking the rising balance.

The fourth jar is titled "SAVE TO KEEP". Put one dime in this jar. Many years from now, your child's working days will be complete, and retirement will step forward to take their place. If he has not "saved to keep", he may face financial hardship.

The animal kingdom knows the importance of saving for the future. While the weather is warm and food is available, the squirrel gathers and stores for the coming winter. He is accumulating for that time, which he knows is approaching, when his savings will be necessary to live.

The Bible gives us a similar example of the ant. "Go to the ant, O sluggard, observe her ways and be wise, which having no chief, officer or ruler, prepares her food in the summer, and gathers her provision in the harvest." (Proverbs 6:6-8)

Teach your child the importance of putting some money aside. Point out to him how his great grandparents can pay for their needs even though they no longer work. Tell him that they have money now because for many years they saved for the future. Your child's fifth dime finds its home in this jar.

The remaining jar is named "SPEND WISELY", and the other five dimes are put there. Discretionary spending is financed from this jar. Your child may use this money any way he wishes, but you should teach him wise spending habits as he uses this money.

When he spends this money like a good steward, give him positive feedback. If he immediately exchanges all his money for candy, let him be "broke" until he earns more discretionary income. It is much less painful to do without candy and toys to learn financial management as a child, than to do without food to learn the same lessons as an adult.

Stewardship is much broader than tithing and wise spending. We stated earlier that it is the process of using everything God has entrusted to us in a manner that is pleasing to

Him. All our possessions should be devoted to furthering God's kingdom.

Children have material possessions that should be taken care of so that they last. After a good steward spends wisely, he uses what he has purchased appropriately. Toys should not be used more roughly than their design allows. Bikes should be used carefully and stored properly. Old clothes should be worn for messy activities. All your child's possessions should be used in a manner that achieves maximum benefit and life.

Time is a possession that requires stewardship. Every person has been given twenty-four hours in each day to serve God and accomplish worldly responsibilities. Time can be used productively or it can be wasted. Guide your child away from time wasters so that he develops proper habits in the use of time. Excessive television is one of the worst time traps to avoid.

Abilities are possessions to be used for God. Children can help adults pick up toys at the end of church. They can sing in their choir and make posters for special events. Children can hold doors for the elderly and pick up communion cups. Using physical abilities to serve God as a child will prepare him to offer his physical, mental, and spiritual abilities as a teenager and adult.

The call for stewardship touches every area of your child's life: his tithe, spending, material assets, time, and abilities. Teach him early in his life that God is pleased when we use resources from His kingdom wisely. Stewardship is not an option in God's eyes. 1 Corinthians 4:2 tells us, *"Moreover it is required in stewards, that a man be found faithful."* Help your child become a faithful steward.

SUMMARY

This chapter has covered post birth activities that make up a plan for spiritual training. Just as a plan is necessary for the athlete who desires a crown of victory for herself, a plan is necessary for the parents who desire the crown of life for their children.

An organized approach to spiritual training instills in your child godly values that she will continue to follow as she grows older. Those values move her in the direction of the cross with the ultimate purpose of securing her salvation. In summary, your child's first five to twelve years should prepare her to say, "Here I am Lord, I am yours!"

SPIRITUAL WARFARE FOR SALVATION

We have completed our look at activities that can be performed before conception, during pregnancy, and following birth that will lay the foundation for securing your child's salvation. As a quick review, they are listed below.

Preconception
1. Experience salvation yourself
2. Put your spiritual life in order
3. Build your faith on God's Word
4. Pray for wisdom
5. Learn to hear from God
6. Be financially ready
7. Pray for your child's physical conception
8. Pray for your child's spiritual conception

Prenatal
1. Lay hands on your baby and pray
2. Read the Bible to your baby
3. Portray an attitude of love not strife
4. Provide an environment of peace and honor of God
5. Walk in faith concerning your child's health and your pregnancy
6. Prepare yourself to take care of your baby's needs

Postpartum
1. Love God with All Her Heart
2. Follow God's Will
3. Keep God's Commandments
4. Love Others as Herself
5. Practice the Fruit of the Spirit
6. Practice Proper Stewardship

The subject of this chapter is the most important part of Securing the Salvation of Your Children. There is a war going on for your children which calls for combat on your part. You must get into the trenches and battle the enemy for the eternal destiny of your children. You must engage in spiritual warfare through intercessory prayer.

If you forget the rest of this book, remember this: TAKE SERIOUSLY, YOUR RESPONSIBILITY TO INTERCEDE FOR THE SALVATION OF YOUR CHILDREN. Spiritual warfare through intercessory prayer is your most effective means to overcome the schemes of the enemy and prepare your child to accept Jesus as Lord.

An interceding parent goes beyond just praying for his children; he prays fervently and earnestly even to the point of travail. An intercessor is one who takes someone's place to plead that person's case before the judge or king. The intercessor's role is like that of the defense attorney, who represents her client before the court to free the client from bondage.

An interceding parent goes before God on behalf of his children to get God's involvement in securing their salvation. That parent represents his children before the court of heaven to free them from the devil's bondage of deception.

The Bible shows a definite connection between spiritual warfare through intercession and resulting salvation. When people pray fervently, the way to eternal life is cleared. Satan's roadblocks are removed and the path to salvation is illuminated.

The Old Testament predicted that travail in prayer would produce spiritual birth, and the New Testament records actual occurrences. Before we discuss those Scriptures, look at some background from the book of Hebrews.

18 For you have not come to a mountain (Sinai) that may be touched and to a blazing fire, and to darkness and gloom and whirlwind,
19 and to the blast of a trumpet and the sound of words which sound was such that those who heard begged that no further word should be spoken to them.
20 For they could not bear the command, "If even a beast touches the mountain, it will be stoned."
21 And so terrible was the sight, that Moses said, "I am full of fear and trembling."
22 But you have come to Mount Zion and to the city of the living God, the heavenly Jerusalem, and to myriads of angels,
23 to the general assembly and church of the first born who are enrolled in heaven, and to God, the Judge of all, and to the spirits of righteous men made perfect,
24 and to Jesus, the mediator of a new covenant, and to the sprinkled blood, which speaks better than the blood of Abel. (Hebrews 12:18-24)

The twelfth chapter of Hebrews describes two historic mountains, Sinai and Zion. Mount Sinai represents the old covenant characterized by the Ten Commandments and animal, blood sacrifice. Mount Zion portrays the new covenant of eternal life through Jesus' shed blood.

The prophet Isaiah looked ahead to Mount Zion to the new covenant of eternal salvation. Notice in Isaiah 66:8, the connection between travail and spiritual birth into salvation. *"Who has heard such a thing? Who has seen such things? Can a land be born in one day? Can a nation be brought forth all at once? As soon as Zion travailed, she also brought forth her sons."* The Old Testament predicted that travail in prayer would produce spiritual birth.

I believe that Zion symbolizes spiritual birth into salvation and that it was Jesus' travail that brought forth sons of the new covenant. Jesus was the original intercessor. He engaged in spiritual warfare on our behalf. His obedience on the cross completed salvation, but the battle was won in the garden of Gethsemane through His travail in prayer. The gospel of Luke records that travail.

39 And He came out and proceeded as was His custom to the Mount of Olives; and the disciples also followed Him.
40 And when He arrived at the place, He said to them, "Pray that you may not enter into temptation."
41 And He withdrew from them about a stone's throw, and He knelt down and began to pray,
42 saying, "Father, if Thou art willing, remove this cup from Me; yet not My will, but Thine be done."
43 Now an angel from heaven appeared to Him, strengthening Him.
44 And being in agony He was praying very fervently; and His sweat became like drops of blood, falling down upon the ground. (Luke 22:39-44)

Jesus prayed fervently about His mission that would bring salvation to a lost world. He represented us before the throne of heaven, and His travail cleared the path to our salvation.

Jesus was the intercessor who bridged the separation between God and men. *"For there is one God, and one mediator also between God and men, the man Christ Jesus who gave Himself as a ransom for all, the testimony borne at the proper time." (1 Timothy 2:5, 6)*

Jesus won the struggle of the cross through prayer in the garden. He travailed and spiritual sons were born as a result. Isaiah had predicted that spiritual warfare would birth sons into the kingdom of God. *"As soon as Zion travailed, she also brought forth her sons." (Isaiah 66:8)* Jesus fulfilled the prophecy.

Spiritual birth through travail in prayer was accomplished by Paul after Jesus left the earth. That fact is important because it shows us that intercession is still the means of birthing spiritual children. Paul was not God or one of the disciples; he was a converted Christian just like we are. If Paul's prayers were part of the salvation process, then our prayers can have the same impact.

An example of Paul's travail is found in his letter to the Galatians. "My little children, of whom I travail in birth again until Christ be formed in you." (Galatians 4:19)

In this passage Paul is praying that the Galatians would grow from childhood to maturity. It states that he is travailing again. Therefore, he must have travailed before. Paul's previous travail was for the Galatians' salvation, resulting in them becoming little children of God. Spiritual warfare, in prayer, was part of their salvation experience.

The enemy is a devourer who roams the earth searching for the vulnerable. 1 Peter 5:8 reads, *"Be of sober spirit, be on the alert. Your adversary, the devil, prowls about like a roaring lion, seeking someone to devour."* Satan's aim is to enslave and ravage all that he can, and he has his eye on your children.

The devil *"prowls about like a roaring lion"*. He does not really have the awesome strength, powerful jaws, or sharp teeth and claws of a lion. He is a pretender and his greatest weapon is deception.

This past weekend I was showing my son how to walk like a duck. That did not make me a duck (although some people watching called me a turkey). Satan walks like a lion, but he is not one. He cannot do anything to prohibit your child from embracing salvation except deceive him and blind his eyes to the message of the gospel.

3 And even if our gospel is veiled, it is veiled to those who are perishing,
4 in whose case the god of this world has blinded the minds of the unbelieving, that they might not see the light of the gospel of the glory of Christ, who is the image of God. (2 Corinthians 4:3, 4)

People remain unsaved because they are blinded to the truth by Satan's deception and lies. The devil plants false ideas that distort reality. He portrays Christianity as a crutch for the weak instead of an entire life support system for the hopeless. He sells sin as being without consequence. For those who are awakening to the message of the gospel, he says, "Consider it tomorrow." His tactic is to place a veil between those who are lost and the light of the gospel. THE FIRST RESPONSIBILITY OF THE INTERCEDING PARENT IS TO THROUGH PRAYER BIND SATAN FROM BLINDING THE MINDS OF HIS CHILDREN.

Have you ever seen the popular game show on television called, "Let's Make a Deal"? At the end of each program, was the most profitable event of the day, "The Big Deal". The two contestants who had won the most valuable prizes during the first part of the show could swap their loot for a chance to participate.

Three curtains were displayed with unseen prizes behind. The individual with the largest previous winnings chose first, followed by the remaining player. Then their choices were revealed by opening the curtains.

Invariably, someone would receive an old bath tub, used garbage cans, or a wrecked car as their final prize. These unwise choices were made because the curtains hid what was behind them. When you cannot see what the selections are, you may make the wrong choice.

"The Big Deal" would have had completely different outcomes if the three curtains had been removed before choices were made. Let me predict the selections. The first person would have picked the prize he wanted the most, the second person would have chosen the better of the other two prizes, and the "zonk" prize would have been avoided. The "Big Deal" would have been an easy game if the curtains were removed.

In the game of "Eternal Life", there are two curtains, heaven and hell, and a choice is mandatory, not optional. Everyone must participate by selecting one of the two curtains. Satan's role is to keep the curtains closed so that people's minds are blinded to the reality of each choice. He prevents individuals from seeing that hell is characterized by eternal suffering and heaven by eternal reward.

If Satan can hide the truth, wrong choices will be made, but if the blinders are removed, the prize of heaven will be selected. The "zonk" of hell will be avoided. "Eternal Life" is an easy game if the curtains are removed.

Satan desires to blind the minds of the unbelieving so that they do not see the light of the gospel. The intercessor combats Satan's efforts by praying for Satan to be bound from veiling the gospel in accordance with Matthew 12:29 and 18:18. "Or how can anyone enter the strongman's house and carry off his property, unless he first binds the strongman? And then he will plunder his house." "Truly I say to you, whatever you shall bind on earth shall have been bound in heaven; and whatever you loose on earth shall have been loosed in heaven."

Intercession binds Satan's attempts to hide the gospel and opens the curtains so that the alternatives can be seen clearly. Obscurity is removed and deception is eliminated. The need for guessing is replaced by the ability to make an enlightened decision. Because intercession cannot force someone to accept Jesus as Savior, people can still select hell for their eternal home, but the chances are unlikely that they will when the curtains are removed.

God wants intercessors who will open the curtains for the lost. He has always looked for intercessors who would pray to change existing circumstances. *"And I searched for a man among them who should build up the wall and stand in the gap before Me for the land, that I should not destroy it; but I found no one." (Ezekiel 22:30)* God wanted a person to pray for His people.

An intercessor who would have stood in the gap between a sinful land and a holy God could have changed the course of events and prevented destruction. Just as God desired an intercessor then to stop the physical destruction of His people, He is calling for prayer warriors now, who will stop the spiritual destruction of our children.

BIND SATAN FROM BLINDING THE MINDS OF YOUR CHILDREN. In the game of "Let's Make a Deal", the impact of a wrong choice is insignificant, but the game of "Eternal Life" is different. The stakes are high and the choice is permanent. The result is either eternal salvation with God or eternal death in hell. Do not let the devil keep the curtains closed.

THE SECOND RESPONSIBILITY OF THE INTERCEDING PARENT IS TO ASK GOD TO REVEAL CLEARLY THE ALTERNATIVES OF HEAVEN AND HELL. When Satan is bound from hiding the gospel, the curtains are left opened, but the choices must be brought out for inspection. It is the work of the Holy Spirit to help display the truth of each choice.

Where Satan is a deceiver, the Holy Spirit discloses the truth. As is the usual case, the things of God and the tactics of Satan are exactly opposite. God utilizes love; Satan hates. God works through faith; Satan operates through fear. God reveals the truth through the Holy Spirit to discredit Satan's deception.

13 "But when He, the Spirit of truth, comes, He will guide you into all the truth; for He will not speak on His own initiative, but whatever He hears, He will speak; and He will disclose to you what is to come.

14 "He shall glorify Me; for He shall take of Mine, and shall disclose it to you.
15 "All things that the Father has are Mine; therefore I said, that He takes of Mine, and will disclose it to you." (John 16:13-15)

The Holy Spirit discloses and describes the prize of heaven and the "zonk" of hell. He is our guide into the truth and makes it possible for the lost to make an enlightened decision concerning their eternal destiny. God speaks the truth; the Holy Spirit hears and relays the message to those willing to listen. He reveals to the lost their separation from God. He also reveals the hope of being adopted into God's family as an heir of the riches of heaven.

16 I do not cease giving thanks for you, while making mention of you in my prayers;
17 that the God of our Lord Jesus Christ, the Father of glory, may give to you a spirit of wisdom and of revelation in the knowledge of Him.
18 I pray that the eyes of your heart may be enlightened, so that you may know what is the hope of His calling, what are the riches of the glory of His inheritance in the saints,
19 and what is the surpassing greatness of His power toward us who believe. These are in accordance with the working of the strength of His might. (Ephesians 1:16-19)

Ask God to send the Holy Spirit to your child to guide him into all the truth. The Holy Spirit can reveal God and Satan for whom they are and disclose the facts concerning heaven and hell so that the right choice can be made. The Holy Spirit can help secure your child's salvation. Once the curtains are opened, the Holy Spirit brings the truth of each choice out for inspection.

The most common way that the Holy Spirit delivers the truth of the gospel is through a person who has already received salvation. That person possesses the truth, and the Holy Spirit assists him in passing the message of eternal life to those who need to hear.

Because the message will be passed verbally from someone who is already a believer to your child, YOUR THIRD RESPONSIBILITY IN SPIRITUAL WARFARE IS TO ASK GOD TO SEND WORKERS TO SHARE THE GOSPEL. In Matthew 9:37-38, Jesus communicated this duty to us. *"Then He said to His disciples, 'The harvest is plentiful, but the workers are few. Therefore, beseech the Lord of the harvest to send out workers into His harvest.'"*

The image is a waving field of golden grain that needs harvesting. The grain invites many reapers and demands haste because one day it will wither away uselessly if a reaper does not attend to it. The harvest is plentiful, but workers are required to bring it in.

The field of grain represents the multitude of people who are lost and who need to be brought into God's kingdom. Your child is part of that field and must be harvested before it is too late. You are the primary reaper, but other workers are necessary to compliment your efforts.

My parents are Christians who took me to church and shared godly principles with me, but it was a visiting pastor who the Holy Spirit used to deliver the truth that spoke directly to me. From his words I understood that Jesus not only died for a lost world, but also that He died for a "lost me". The Holy Spirit sent the truth to me through a worker who was available to harvest the lost.

The available Christian, who is willing to be a worker to harvest children into God's kingdom, can share the gospel by describing the choices of eternal life and eternal death from a personal view point. The people to whom I am most grateful are those who loved me enough to allow God to deliver the truth through them. They simply passed on to me what was passed on to them.

The summer Olympics always includes relay races as part of the track and field events. Those races are sometimes won or lost at the point where the baton is passed from one person to another. A successful transfer is crucial to the continuation of the race.

The continuation of God's kingdom is dependent on the successful transfer of the baton of salvation. You have probably heard it said that the extinction of Christianity is always only one generation away. If no one in the next generation ever heard the good news, Christianity would die.

Workers willing to share the gospel message are an important part of your child's salvation. Pray regularly to the Lord of the harvest asking Him to send laborers to assist you in harvesting your child.

We have looked at three parental responsibilities in carrying out spiritual warfare for our children's salvation:

(1) Bind Satan from blinding their minds to the gospel,
(2) Ask God to reveal the truth through the Holy Spirit, and
(3) Ask God to send workers to help harvest your children.

YOUR FOURTH RESPONSIBILITY IS TO ASK GOD TO DRAW YOUR CHILD TO BE ADOPTED INTO GOD'S FAMILY. At birth we are not natural children of God. We must be adopted through our acceptance of Jesus as Savior and Lord. God draws your child, and if he follows God's leading, he is adopted into full family privileges. The following two Scriptures show the drawing and adoption process.

"No one can come to Me, unless the Father who sent Me draws him; and I will raise him up on the last day." (John 6:44)

For you have not received a spirit of slavery leading to fear again, but you have received a spirit of adoption as sons by which we cry out, "Abba! Father!" (Romans 8:15)

Spiritual warfare through intercessory prayer is crucial to the salvation process. When godly men and women travail, spiritual babies are born. Spiritual warfare will bind Satan from blinding your child to the gift of salvation and will enable your child to see the reality of heaven versus hell. It will employ workers to harvest him and will cause him to be drawn into adoption as a child of God.

Take seriously your responsibility to intercede for the salvation of your child. The stakes are very high, and his choice will be permanent throughout eternity. Be persistent in spiritual warfare; demand that Satan take his blinders off your child. Boldly entreat God to give your child every chance to accept salvation. Push through. Do not quit. Fight as if your child's life depended on it; because it does.

There was a pastor who was praying one afternoon, and the name, Charles Rogers, came to his mind. He was urged to intercede fervently for Mr. Rogers which he was obedient to do. The pastor found himself binding Satan and death. After several minutes, there was a release of the burden, and a sense that everything was taken care of swept over him.

Two weeks later the pastor was invited out of town to preach on intercessory prayer and soul winning. After one service he went to a restaurant with the pastor of the church where the meetings were being held. A woman came up to their table and asked if they would go to the hospital and pray for her father. He was in a coma and was not expected to live.

The pastors said they would make the requested visit and inquired as to the man's name. "Charles Rogers" was the reply.

This was the same name that came to the pastor's mind during prayer.

The rest of this success story had already been accomplished during the spiritual warfare of prayer. The men went to the hospital, and the visiting pastor spoke to Charles Rogers. "Mr. Rogers, God spoke your name to me two weeks ago and I interceded for you. There was a release in my spirit that God was raising you up. Now get up." Mr. Rogers squeezed the pastor's hand, opened his eyes from the coma, got up out of bed, checked out, and went home.

Not only does intercession change physical death to life, but also it converts spiritual death into spiritual life. There was another pastor who invited some members of his congregation to his home for refreshments. As the drinks and food were being prepared, a strong urge to pray came over the pastor. He asked his guests to pray with him, which they did for over an hour. They were praying for an unnamed person who was spiritually dead.

At the end of the prayer time, God gave the pastor a vision of himself preaching a sermon which he had never preached. At the invitation he saw himself lean over the pulpit, point to a man, and say, "You are over seventy years old and have been brought up to believe there is no hell. You have one foot in hell, and the other one is slipping in." The man got up from his second row seat and came forward to be saved.

The pastor told his company exactly what he had seen, what the man was wearing, and where he was sitting. The next Sunday that man came in and sat in the second row. The pastor preached the sermon from the vision, leaned over the pulpit, pointed, and spoke to the man. The man came forward to be saved.

The man remarked to the pastor, "You said I am over seventy, I am seventy-two. This is the first time I have ever been inside a Christian church. You said I was brought up to believe that there is no hell and that is correct. My parents were Universalists who taught me that hell does not exist. You said I had one foot in hell, and the other was slipping. You were right. I almost died from a heart attack, and my health is poor."

God found an intercessor who was willing to pray for spiritual life and salvation resulted. The man may have come forward on Sunday night, but it was accomplished a few days earlier in prayer.

You can accomplish the same thing through spiritual warfare for your children. Be consistent and persistent in your intercession for them. Do not relax during battle because the enemy will not take a break. Force Satan's deception to be ineffective so that your children can make enlightened choices.

The following poem, whose author is not known, relates the impact that an interceding parent can have.

MOTHER'S ELBOWS ON MY BED
"I was but a youth and thoughtless,
As all youths are apt to be;
Though I had a Christian mother
Who had taught me carefully,
But there came a time when pleasure
Of the world came to allure,
And I no more sought the guidance
Of her love so good and pure.
Her tender admonitions fell
But lightly on my ear,
And for the gentle warnings
I felt an inward sneer.
How could I prove my manhood
Were I not firm of will?
No threat of future evil
Should all my pleasure kill.
But mother would not yield her boy
To Satan's sinful sway,
And though I spurned her counsel
She knew a better way.
No more she tried to caution
Of ways she knew were vain,
And though I guessed her heartache
I could not know its pain.
She made my room an altar,
A place of secret prayer,
And there she took her burden
And left it in His care.
And morning, noon and evening
By that humble bedside low,
She sought the aid of Him Who
Best can understand a mother's woe.
And I went my way unheeding,
Careless of the life I led,
Until one day I noticed
Prints of elbows on my bed.
Then I saw that she had been there
Praying for her wayward boy,

Who for love of worldly pleasure
Would her peace of mind destroy.
While I wrestled with my conscience,
Mother wrestled still in prayer,
Till that little room seemed hallowed
Because so oft she met Him there.
With her God she held the fortress,
And though not a word she said,
My stubborn heart was broken
By those imprints on my bed.
Long the conflict raged within me,
Sin against my mother's prayers.
Sin MUST YIELD for MOTHER NEVER
While she daily met Him there.
And her constant love and patience
Were like coals upon my head,
Together with the imprints
Of her elbows on my bed.
Mother love and God love
Are a combination rare,
And one that can't be beaten
When sealed by earnest prayer.
And so, at last the fight was won,
And I to Christ was led,
And mother's prayers were answered
By her elbows on my bed."
Unknown.

Spiritual warfare through intercessory prayer is your mo
effective means to overcome the schemes of the enemy ar
prepare your child to accept Jesus as Lord. FULFILL YOU
RESPONSIBILITY TO PRAY TO SECURE YOUR CHILD'S SALVATION.

THE PLAN OF SALVATION

13 Whoever will call upon the name of the Lord will be saved.
14 How then shall they call upon Him in whom they have not believed? And how shall they believe in Him whom they have not heard? And how shall they hear without a preacher? (Romans 10:13, 14)

As promised in the Bible, every child that calls upon the name of Jesus for salvation will be saved. We have looked at four chapters of activities that point a child in the right direction and clear the road to eternal life. All those activities prepare your child to hear and accept God's plan of salvation and proclaim Jesus as Lord.

Romans 10:9-10 reads, "that if you confess with your mouth Jesus as Lord, and believe in your heart that God raised Him from the dead, you shall be saved; for with the heart man believes, resulting in righteousness, and with the mouth he confesses, resulting in salvation."

Before your child can believe in his heart and confess with his mouth, he must hear with his ears. *"And how shall they believe in Him whom they have not heard?"* Your child cannot believe in Jesus and His work on the cross if he never hears.

For your child to hear, someone must "preach" the plan of salvation to him. *"And how shall they hear without a preacher?"* That preacher is you. When you explain the salvation message, he hears which makes it possible for him to believe.

The steps of the salvation process are as follows:
(1) Your child is prepared to hear through the activities of the first four chapters.
(2) You intercede for your child's salvation.
(3) Your child hears as you take the role of the preacher and present the plan of salvation.
(4) Your child believes the gospel in her or his heart.
(5) Your child confesses verbally the decision to accept Jesus as Lord.
(6) Your child's salvation is secured.

(Prepare-intercede-hear-believe-confess-salvation)

Steps one and two of the process call for five to twelve years of preparation that brings your child to the threshold of eternal life. As he: (1) Hears God's Word, (2) Grows in an environment of love, (3) Learns godly principles through spiritual training, and (4) Receives the benefits of spiritual warfare through your prayers, he arrives at a decision point.

Steps three through six are the wrap up of securing his salvation. Five to twelve years of foundation have brought your child to these thirty minutes of hearing and deciding. Sure, he has heard the gospel before, but there will come a point, because of your preparation, that he will realize the he is required to make decision in the game of Eternal Life. He must choose between heaven and hell. Your years of effort can make his choice easy.

The Index following this chapter provides links to various presentations of the plan of salvation. All have the same central truth. Man is headed toward hell because of sin, but Jesus provided a way to heaven that we can choose. The choice is ours but God demands a decision.

The presentations differ in content and intellectual level. Some presentations can be understood by young children, and other presentations are for teenagers or adults. All, however, can be adapted to the maturity and understanding of a specific child.

Again, preparation is the key. Choose a plan of salvation that you feel comfortable with and learn it. Practice presenting to someone until it flows naturally. Use it during everyday life to share the good news with lost people. During the five to twelve years you are preparing your child to hear and believe, become proficient at relating the truths of salvation to the perishing.

Let me close our study by urging you to share my passion for lost children. Do not let them wander through this life choosing to be separated from God in the next life. Do not cause them to ask, "Why didn't you tell me?"

Your child is a player in the game of Eternal Life. The stakes are high, and the choice is permanent. Do all you can prepare him to choose heaven and avoid hell. Do all you can bring him into God's Kingdom. Do all you can to secure his salvation.

CONCLUSION

There is a tendency in America today for Christian parents to turn over many of the responsibilities concerning their children to other adults. Day care workers serve as stand in parents who have had much of the rearing process passed on to them. In doing so, the shaping of our children's morals and social skills is largely out of our control.

This passing of responsibilities is not limited to moral and social training only. We have handed down our children's religious training in the same manner. Our church teachers have become our children's primary source of information about God and Christian values. Those few minutes of training each week are not enough.

I am not saying that day care workers and church teachers are unqualified, but I do want to say that Christian parents need to take an active role in the child training process. Our precious children have been entrusted to us for a short while, and we will be accountable to God for our efforts in training them to be Christ like.

Children are a valuable resource to God. They are the only hope of continuation of His Kingdom. A little boy is the only thing God can use to make a man, and a little girl is the only thing God can use to make a woman.

"Train up a child in the way he should go, even when he is old he will not depart from it." (Proverbs 22:6)

It is your responsibility to do the training. It is your responsibility to teach your children to be Christ-like. It is your responsibility to commit to be an active part of "SECURING THE SALVATION OF YOUR CHILDREN."

APPENDIX A: PRESENTATIONS OF THE PLAN OF SALVATION

This index contains three presentations of the plan of salvation.

(1) The Four Spiritual Laws
http://www.4laws.com/laws/english/default.htm

(2) The Bridge Presentation
http://www.discipleshipint.org/#/resources/the-bridge-illustration

(3) The ABC Presentation
https://www.teenmissions.org/resources/abcs-salvation

There are many more presentations, but these are three of the most widely used.

Made in the USA
Columbia, SC
03 June 2018